S0-BFD-195

"HUMOR OVER EASY, SPICED WITH LAUGHTER."
—*South Bend Tribune*

—When feeding baby, forget strained spinach, try applesauce—it blends better with the wallpaper.

—Only a mother can understand how a budget that cannot tolerate a winter coat for herself can come up with enough cash to send her high school senior on a ski trip.

—When investing in the stock market, it will make no difference if you "buy high" or "buy low"; once that stock realizes it's *yours*, it will sink into oblivion.

—Given a five-dollar bill and sent to the store for a three-fifty purchase, eight out of ten children will account for the change as follows: (a) "I lost it," (b) "The man didn't give me any change," (c) "I thought you said I could buy some candy and soda." Two out of ten will never get to the store, and on returning home will ask, "What five dollars?"

"AMERICA'S EXPERT ON SEEING THE HUMOROUS SIDE OF RAISING A FLOCK OF CHILDREN IS AT IT AGAIN!"
—*The Monitor*

TERESA BLOOMINGDALE's previous books include *Life Is What Happens When You're Making Other Plans*, *Murphy Must Have Been a Mother*, *Up a Family Tree*, and *I Should Have Seen It Coming When the Rabbit Died*. The wife of insurance executive A. Lee Bloomingdale, she has written numerous columns for leading newspapers, lectured nationwide, and made hundreds of television and radio appearances.

SENSE
AND
MOMSENSE

*the wisdom possessed by a seasoned mother
and the ability to laugh at marriage and family
foibles—*after* learning how to survive it all!

by
Teresa Bloomingdale

A SIGNET BOOK

NEW AMERICAN LIBRARY

SIGNET TRADEMARK REG. U.S. PAT. OFF. AND FOREIGN COUNTRIES
REGISTERED TRADEMARK—MARCA REGISTRADA
HECHO EN CHICAGO, U.S.A.

SIGNET, SIGNET CLASSIC, MENTOR, ONYX, PLUME, MERIDIAN and NAL BOOKS are published by NAL PENGUIN INC., 1633 Broadway, New York, New York 10019

First Signet Printing, May, 1987

1 2 3 4 5 6 7 8 9

PRINTED IN THE UNITED STATES OF AMERICA

To Mary Helen
Artie
Madeleine
Betsy
and
Janet

From your loving sister

CONTENTS

CONTENTS

Part Two

BACK TO THE BASICS . . .
OR FORWARD? 55

Part Three
IT'S ALL IN THE GAME 87

Contents

Part Four

THREE CHEERS FOR
THE MSS.! 125

Part Five

POTPOURRI 145

Part Six

OOOO . . . THERE'S A BUG IN MY BOOK! 187

CONTENTS

I would like to thank the second-grade students of Loveland School in Omaha, along with their teachers, Judy Perry and Patricia Newland, and the second-grade students of Sunset Hills School, and their teacher, Kathy Drozda, for their help with the chapter "When I Grow Up . . ."

INTRODUCTION

What is "momsense"?

Momsense, Webster's Collegiate Dictionary would tell us, if Webster had ever taken time out to listen to his mom, is language or ideas intelligible only to mothers.

For example, it may make no sense at all to a sixteen-year-old boy when his mother says, "You must have the car home by midnight; I don't want any accidents." Doesn't she know that there are fewer accidents after midnight than before?

Of course she knows that, but she will also argue that there might well be one fewer if he is not driving around out there tempting fate. That's just good momsense.

As a mother of ten children, I consider myself somewhat of an expert on momsensical ideas, a few of which I mention here:

1. All little children know that when Mom gets chilly, everybody puts on a sweater, and when Mom gets tired, everybody takes a nap. But only teenagers realize that when Mom is on a diet, everybody starves.

2. If a month-old baby is taking most of her formula at every other feeding, a mother suffering from post-partum exhaustion may, in all good conscience, ignore the 2 A.M. howling. (In 99 percent of the cases, when parents claim that "baby is sleeping through the night," it means that *they* are sleeping through the night.)

3. A four-year-old who deliberately sasses his father, disobeys his mother, and drives his grandma up the wall is begging for punishment. Don't deny him.

4. Contrary to what sociologists say, it is permissible to spank a toddler if, for the third time in ten minutes, he has (a) run out into the street, (b) kicked the cat, (c) bitten his baby sister. (Though I hasten to add that spankings should hurt nothing except the feelings.)

5. One bad report card does not mean the end of the world. (Two, on the other hand, just might.)

6. It makes perfect sense that a mother who can remember your first words, what you wore to your kindergarten Halloween party, and all three verses of a poem you wrote in sixth grade cannot remember if you had any telephone calls this afternoon while you were out job-hunting.

7. Only a mother can understand how a budget that cannot tolerate a winter coat for herself can come up with enough cash to send her high school senior on a ski trip.

8. Jazz, swing, and boogie-woogie are *music*; rock is *noise*.

9. Christmas programs, music recitals, and sports events are more important than board meetings, golf tournaments, and gallbladder operations. (I have postponed a gallbladder operation so many times, my gallstones gave up and went away.)

10. Vacations are cheaper than psychiatrists.

11. If you want to please your mother, talk to her. If you want to make points with your father, listen to him.

12. God allows children to suffer the heartaches of lost toys, poor report cards, fender benders, broken prom dates, sorority/fraternity rejections, and acne so that when they become parents they will understand why their children are *miserable*.

Part One

BLOOMINGDALE'S BOARDING HOUSE

1

ASK ANY GRANDMA

A lot of people assume that because I am the mother of ten children I must be an expert on motherhood, but such is not the case. It is true that I have learned a great deal over the years, but fortunately I have managed to forget most of what I have learned. (That is how I stayed sane.)

Since I have become a grandmother, however, certain memories have surfaced, and while they are still fresh in my mind I would like to answer those questions I am so often asked by young parents.

Q. "We just got married. How long should we wait before we have our first baby?"

A. Let us hope . . . nine months.

Q. "Our baby is ten weeks old. When will he roll over?"

A. The first time you put him on your bed and dash to the nursery for a clean diaper. (And once they go, they go. The first time one of our sons rolled over, he rolled off the bed, across the room, out the door, and down the steps. Never trust a baby.)

Q. "When will our baby walk?"

A. When he is approximately three months older than his little cousin was when she walked. (This is not to say that girl babies are quicker than boy babies; it's just that mothers who turn into aunts tell lies a lot.)

Q. "Should we get our baby a pacifier?"

A. Why? Doesn't he have thumbs? Pacifiers are harmless, but if you buy one, buy ten. There's nothing worse than not being able to find the baby's pacifier.

Q. "When will Baby say his first word?"

A. When he's at the babysitter's, and she won't remember what it was. (In deference to modern families, psychologists have decided that "first words" and "first steps" unwitnessed by a parent, grandparent, or sibling don't count.)

Q. "How long should we let Baby stay on the bottle?"

A. If he's pouring his own, hand him a cup.

Q. "My mother-in-law is very possessive; she wants me to bring the baby to see her at least three times a week, and leave him there all day long. What should I tell her?"

A. "Thank you."

Q. "What shall I tell our toddler who wants to stay up past her bedtime?"

A. The same thing I tell my teenager who wants to stay *out* past *my* bedtime: "No!" (Practice this word; you'll use it a lot.)

Q. "What are your views on day care centers?"

A. I'm glad I don't run one.

Q. "At what age should a toddler stop taking a nap?"

A. When his mother no longer needs one.

Q. "I can't get our baby to eat strained spinach; he spits it out all over the place!"

A. I'd spit it out too; try applesauce.

Q. "Does applesauce taste better? Does it have more vitamins? Is it more filling?"

A. No. But it blends better with the wallpaper.

Q. "How does a new mother get any sleep?"

A. Sleep? Sleep? What's that?

Q. "Our firstborn is almost four years old. Should we have another baby this year?"

A. Oh, absolutely! This year, and next year, and the year after that! (I feel it only fair to remind you that these questions are being answered by a grandmother.)

2

"MY MOMMY HAS LINES IN HER FACE!"

With so many women now combining marriage and a career, there is an ongoing controversy concerning the ideal age to have children. While women have traditionally had children in their twenties (the women are in their twenties, not the children, though that might not be a bad idea), the modern mother is opting to establish her career first, and to put off having children until she is in her mid- or even late thirties.

As a mother who has done it all (and I do mean *all;* four babies in my twenties, six in my thirties, and a career in the midst of the muddle), I have come to the conclusion that the ideal age to have children is fourteen.

The most competent "mother" I ever met was not a mother at all, but a fourteen-year-old "mother's helper" who could handle my kids as easily as she could paperdolls. Marcene was not only quicker, brighter, and stronger than my kids, she was also close enough to their age to anticipate their every prank. (Coincidentally, Marcene is now a young professional putting off marriage and motherhood until her thirties. I'd like to think that it is her busy career as a physician and surgeon that influenced her decision to postpone motherhood, and not her memory of my mischievous children.)

Since society frowns on motherhood at fourteen, and nature intervenes after forty, motherhood is pretty much limited to the twenties and thirties. But which should it be?

Both have positive aspects. At twenty-five a mother has more energy, strength, and stamina, but at thirty-five she has more wisdom, self-confidence, and money, which, let's face it, is nice to have at any age.

But they both have negative aspects as well. The midtwenties mother will feel that the whole world has run off without her, while the midthirties mother will think she has fallen into a time warp. Where are all the women her age?

Certainly not where she is. I know. I have checked into maternity wards where the other mothers looked like little girls playing "pregnant." I have been to PTA meetings which I mistook for a gathering of cheerleaders. And I have gone to graduations where it was assumed that I was the graduate's grandmother.

Before you opt for midthirties motherhood, I suggest you consider the following:

1. Your parents. If you think they nagged you to get married, just wait till they get on your case about grandchildren.

2. Can you really trust an obstetrician who was in kindergarten when you were in college?

3. Are you prepared to explain, again and again, that you are not this kid's grandmother?

4. Will it bother you when your first-grader wants to take you to show-and-tell because nobody will believe that his mommy has lines in her face?

5. Thirty-nine years after the fact, can you remember how to do third-grade arithmetic?

6. When your friends are going on Caribbean cruises, will you be content going on campouts with the Cub Scouts?

7. Can you possibly imagine the frustration of trying to teach a little kid to tie his shoes when you are wearing bifocals?

8. Do you think a midlife crisis can survive (a) teaching a teenager to drive, (b) chaperoning a high school dance, (c) reading college transcripts?

9. Do you plan on paying that college tuition with your Social Security benefits?

10. Do you want to be a grandma when you are too old to enjoy it?

Don't wait; start young! But I must warn you: Babies are addictive. You may end up with ten.

3

THE GUILT COMPLEX

I will never understand my children. For the first fifteen years of their lives they refused to take the blame for anything, no matter how damaging the evidence against them, but after they pass age sixteen, whenever anything goes wrong, they automatically assume it is their fault. This seems to be particularly true when they are involved in an auto accident. No matter what the circumstances, the first thing they do, after the impact, is pop out of the car and shout, "Oh, I am so sorry! It was all my fault!" They are an insurance adjuster's delight.

Just the other night our daughter came home and announced that she had had another fender bender. After assuring us that nobody was hurt, she said, "I'm really sorry; this was all my fault."

"Did you get a ticket?" asked her father, and she replied:

"No; the accident happened in the theater parking lot, and the driver of the other car said there wasn't any point in our calling the police."

"You'd better give me the details," said my husband in his most long-suffering tone.

"Well," said our daughter, "I had just come out of the movie and was walking across the parking lot when I saw this man leaning over our car. I thought at first he might be a car thief, but then I realized that he had just crashed his car into ours and he was putting a note on my windshield."

"Wait a minute," said my husband, "if our car was parked, and you weren't even around at the time of the accident, how could it have been your fault?"

"You sound just like the other driver, Dad," said our daughter. "He didn't think it was my fault either, until I explained to him that I probably should have pulled our car further into the parking space. Then he agreed that I was to blame."

"I'll bet he did," said my husband. "What's the guy's name?"

"I don't know," said our daughter. "I didn't ask him."

"Well look on the note!" said her father.

"I don't have it," she said. "He said since he didn't have any damage to his car, and we agreed it was my fault, he might as well tear up the note."

That was when my husband exploded.

"Do you mean to tell me that you were involved in an automobile accident and you didn't even get the other guy's name? Didn't you learn in Driver's Education that you must get the other guy's name, address, license number, and insurance company? And how many times have I told you never, ever say it was your fault. Always assume it was the other guy's fault, and we will work out the facts later."

"You're asking me to make false accusations, Dad,"

said our sanctimonious daughter, "and I simply cannot do that."

"SINCE WHEN?" shouted her father. "When your toys got broken, you blamed your brothers! When your bike got stolen, you blamed your sister! When you flunked algebra, you blamed your teacher! Nothing was ever your fault; now suddenly, when it's going to cost me money, everything's your fault! Don't be so quick to take the blame! Be assertive! Accuse before you are accused; you'll find that most of the time you'll get away with it!"

"I'm glad to hear you say that, Dad," she said, "because when I pulled into the driveway just now, I didn't notice that you had parked your car at an angle and I sort of brushed up against the front fender. We'll forget about it this time, but from now on, watch the way you park, okay?"

Needless to say, this was not one of those times.

4

GUESSING THE AGE

The other evening our new neighbors strolled over to our backyard patio to introduce themselves, and in the course of the conversation their teenage daughter bounded into our yard, asked her dad for the car keys, and bounded out again.

"I apologize for our daughter," said the embarrassed father. "She should have said hello and introduced herself. That was Lucy; she's sixteen."

"I guessed," I said.

"Guessed what?" he asked.

"That Lucy is sixteen," I said. "Sixteen is the only age that asks for car keys. Before that age they don't need them, and after that age they have their own set, if not their own car."

At that moment, our youngest son came out on the patio and asked my husband to lend him five dollars.

" 'Lend'?" asked my husband with a laugh. "What's with this 'lend'? Can I believe I will ever get this back?"

"Someday, Dad," said our son, pocketing the five-dollar bill. "If I ever get a job. I can't wait to go to work!"

"Is he fifteen?" asked our neighbor after our son had left.

"Yes," I said. "How did you know?"

"Because at fourteen they are still saying 'Gimme,' not 'Lend me,' and at sixteen they usually have a job and are complaining that they can't wait to retire!"

This led us into a discussion of typical comments indicative of age, such as the following:

"Can I get up now, Mama? Is it *finally* morning?" (Everybody under the age of five.)

"It *can't* be morning already! Lemme sleep five more minutes!" (Everybody over the age of five.)

"I just love school!" (First-grader—first week of school.)

"School! Blaggh!" (Ever after . . . until first week away at college.)

"Are you and Daddy going out to dinner? Why can't I go with you?" (Age six.)

"Go to dinner with you? Do I have to?" (Age sixteen.)

"Can I get an argyle sweater, Daddy, please, please, please? Every girl in school has one but me!" (Age fourteen.)

"Nice sweater, Mom, but I hope you don't expect me to wear it to school. Every girl in my class has one exactly like it." (Age seventeen.)

"Aw, Mom, these pants are okay! Anyway, I haven't got time to change; I've gotta be at the ballpark in ten minutes!" (Boy, age eleven, on the fourth day in the same pair of jeans.)

"Don't rush me, Mother; I have to change my clothes." (Girl, age fifteen, who has changed outfits four times since breakfast.)

"But Dad, I just took a bath last Tuesday!" (Boy, ten, and it was a week ago Tuesday.)

"Hurry up in there! I gotta wash my hair!" (Boy, seventeen, who hasn't shampooed in six hours.)

"I am seriously considering dropping out of school, getting a full-time job, and moving into my own place." (Age eighteen, usually during college midterm exams.)

"What do you mean, am I ever gonna get out of college, get a job, and find an apartment? What's the hurry?" (Age twenty-five, after changing his major, again.)

"My dad's the smartest man in the whole, wide world!" (Age three to twelve.)

"You think *your* dad's dumb, you should meet mine!" (Thirteen to nineteen.)

"I'll ask my dad; *he'll* know." (Ever after.)

"Mommy, why do you and Daddy go out so much? You're *never* home!" (Age ten, to parents who go out one night a month . . . maybe.)

"Hey, Dad, why don't you ever take Mom anyplace? You guys are such drags!" (Age eighteen, to parents who go out twice a week, at least.)

"Please, Parents dear, stop treating me like a child. You must realize that I am an adult now, old enough to make my own decisions, to do my own thing. You have to let go!" (Age nineteen.)

"Pay part of my own tuition? Gimme a break! You're my parents! You've got a responsibility to educate me!" (Same child, same age, possibly even same day.)

"Please, Mama, let me help you with those dishes!" (Age four.)

I have been told that this offer may be repeated at a later age, but the only documented case I could find was one in St. Joseph, Missouri, where a mother claims her daughter insists on helping with the dinner dishes every night of the week. The daughter's age? Fifty-eight.

5

MARGARET MARY, WHERE ARE YOU?

I have yet to meet her in person, but I have already decided that she would be an ideal daughter-in-law. She called here the other night to speak to one of our sons, and instead of mumbling, " 'S Tim there?" as so many of his callers do, she said cheerfully:

"Hi, Mrs. Bloomingdale! This is Margaret Mary O'Rourke. May I please speak to Tim?"

Ah, what a courteous young person! Her mother must be so proud!

For years I have been trying to teach my children telephone courtesy, but I am about ready to give up in despair. I don't understand them. They know how to meet and greet people in person; I am always proud of their poise and charm when I entertain guests at home. It is only on the phone that they become mumble-mouthed morons.

I will hear them dial the phone, then ask, " 'S Mary there?" or worse, "Lemme talk to Mary." And should Mary's mother dare to ask who is calling, my charming, personable, intelligent son will mutter:

"Forget it. I'll call her later."

Anonymity is cherished. You'd think we were members of the mob. I have told my children again and again that when they phone someone, they should give their name, then ask for the person to whom they wish to speak, then if the person is not there, leave a polite, clear message. And if they really want to impress somebody's parents, they should make a little polite conversation.

They look at me as if I'm out of my mind, and continue to go nameless.

They are just as bad, if not worse, when they answer the phone. It is polite and acceptable, I tell them, to offer a simple "Hello," but it would be even better to answer the phone by saying, "This is the Such-and-Such residence, So-and-So, or Whoever speaking; may I help you?"

I should have stopped at the "Hello."

The next time one of our sons answered the phone, he said, "This is the Such-and-Such residence; who do you want to talk to: So-and-So or Whomever?"

It's not just the boys. The girls are just as bad. But they don't mumble; they shout. And they always answer with the same formula: "Love Station KEZO! . . . Did I win? Did I win?" (It's not as bad as it used to be, however; during the CB-radio craze, our oldest son invariably answered the phone with: "You've got a ten-two, Mr. Magoo; you're wall-to-wall and ten feet tall; we've got our ears on here. What's your handle?" We suffered at least three years of CB slanguage.)

When Margaret Mary O'Rourke called again last night, I decided to use her as an example. I suggested to our sons that they be as polite and cheerful, as clear and concise, as that lovely Margaret Mary. What a charming girl! My only criticism of her is that she calls so often; two or three times a night, in fact.

At that point my daughter could take it no longer.

"Oh, come off it, Mom; you've been had," she said, and then the truth came out.

It seems that my sons, knowing how impressed I am with telephone courtesy (and how prejudiced I am in favor of the Irish) told *all* their girls to use the name Margaret Mary O'Rourke when they call. In this way, the girls can retain their anonymity, and the boys can retain their privacy.

But someplace out there, there must be a real Margaret Mary, in character and courtesy if not in actual name and nationality, and I just want all you prospective mothers-in-law to know: I've got ABC dibs on her!

6

MY SON THE POWER BROKER

When my oldest son was little, he vowed, each Christmas, that he would someday make his fortune selling batteries door-to-door the day after Christmas. I have no doubt that, had he ever bothered to pursue this idea, he not only could have put himself through college, but retired immediately thereafter. As it turned out, he forsook the promising battery business for a succesful career in insurance, where he is making almost enough money to keep his own child in battery-operated toys and toothbrushes.

My youngest son, still in high school and facing the prospect of college, law school, and (let us hope) working for a living, shares his older brother's youthful enthusiasm for making money quick in the battery business. However, his idea is not to sell batteries, but to eliminate them.

He says he is going to open a Santa's Workshop featuring not just toys, but gifts for all the family. The common feature of these items will be the fact that not one of them will require batteries, adapters, plugs, or power of any kind, including solar.

His family gifts include:

For Mom: A portable mixer that beats, whips, stirs, blends, and splatters the kitchen counter as efficiently as any electric model. An attractive feature of this mixer is a nondetachable twin beater which need never be wrenched from the handle for rinsing or washing; just toss the whole appliance into the dishwasher. (If this powerless mixer bears a remarkable resemblance to the old-fashioned eggbeater, nobody under the age of sixty will notice.)

For Dad: A nonrechargeable, no-plug razor that comes complete without batteries or AC-DC adapter. This razor has a lifetime blade that can be kept permanently sharp simply by swishing it occasionally along the accompanying leather strop. An enticing feature of this razor is the guarantee that your adolescent son won't steal or even borrow it, for no adolescent today can figure out how to work anything that doesn't have an on-off switch.

For Junior: A portable, powerless nonvideo game (with a lifetime warranty). Incredible as it may seem, this game (a) has no batteries or power attachment, (b) need not be attached to a television, typewriter, or computer temninal, (c) does not go BLEEP-BLEEP, PING-PING, RAT-A-TAT, or, in fact, make any noise at all. (I understand that the patent for the silence factor is pending.) The game consists of a simple, squared board and thirty-two coin-sized disks, sixteen red and sixteen black. The purpose of this two-player game is for each player to advance his disks in an effort to occupy the other's space. My son suggests calling the game checkers; rather catchy, don't you think? (He also has an idea for a real estate game in which play money would be used to buy houses, hotels, railroads, and utilities in an attempt to monopolize the market, but I told him it would never sell.)

For Sis: A self-powered wristwatch. (The "self" being Sis, who, by simply twisting the tiny watch-stem each day, can keep the watch going indefinitely.) This watch is a real conversation piece in that it is not digital; instead, it has a round "face" circled by numbers one to twelve, and two arrowed "hands," a short one to indicate the hour and a longer one to note the minutes. (Not recommended for persons under sixteen, unless you are prepared to spend most of Christmas Day teaching them how to "tell time.")

For Little Brother: A super-speed, easy-to-assemble toy train. No power packs, no plugs, no transformers, shrill whistles, or blinking lights to burn out, this simple-to-set-up (just hook the cars together and away it goes!) train will go as fast or as slow as the child pushing it. (Comes complete with track; child not included.)

For Baby Sister: A No-Tears Tessie doll. Tearless Tessie not only promises not to cry, neither will she eat, drink, talk, walk, sing a song, or wet her pants. Tessie will just lie in her cradle, smiling her dimpled smile, and wait patiently to be picked up and hugged. (An exciting feature of the Tessie doll is her lack of birth certificate, adoption papers, extra clothes, or other unwanted accessories, including a boyfriend.)

I told my son that I thought his ideas were excellent and he really should get right to work on them.

"Can't," he said with a yawn. "It's time for my nap. I gotta recharge my batteries, you know!"

No, I didn't know, but I suppose I should have suspected.

7

MOTHER'S DAY

Mother's Day has come and gone and many mothers are in a blue funk because they didn't get a single gift, or even a phone call, from their children.

Not me. I am wallowing in gifts and exhausted from visiting with my still-at-home children as well as those living away from home, all of whom came to see me, bringing along their spouses, children, and gifts for dear old Mom.

My children never forget Mother's Day, thanks to a few hints my mother taught me long ago, not the least of which is:

Remind them. "It is a mother's obligation," my mother used to say, "to train children in the finer things of life, one of the finest being to remember their mother on Mother's Day." Two weeks or so before Mother's Day, it is a good idea to post reminders around the house. (Never rely on your children's memories, and for heaven's sake, don't rely on their father's; he can't even remember Father's Day.)

The obvious place to post a reminder is the refrigerator door, which will alert even those children who are living away from home because the fact that they have moved out doesn't mean they have lost interest in your refrigerator. However, some children don't read refrigerator doors, as they all too often bear such best-ignored messages as dental appointments or calls from a teacher inquiring about the whereabouts (or even the existence of) a term paper. In lieu of the refrigerator, therefore, I recommend mirrors as message centers, for never in the history of offspring has a child, teenager, or young adult passed a mirror without pausing a moment for self-appraisal.

Talk About It. Sometimes a written reminder of Mother's Day is not enough. In this case, you must go the verbal route. Talk about it.

In talking about Mother's Day, you can be either devious or obvious. The devious method is to mention how sorry you feel for your friend Gloria because those thoughtless children of hers will undoubtedly forget Mother's Day, which, coincidentally, just happens to fall two days after Mulhall's has their sale on rosebushes. The obvious method is to say, "Mulhall's is having a sale on rosebushes; I'd like two for Mother's Day."

Or better yet, call Mulhall's, order the rosebushes, and have them send the bill to your kids.

Talk Around It. If you think it is too direct to suggest gifts for yourself for Mother's Day, ask your kids' advice on what to give their grandmother for Mother's Day. (This will not only jog their memory, it may also bring you some much needed ideas, for as we all know, grandmas have everything and need nothing, while mothers have nothing and need everything.)

Plan for It. If you expect your toddlers to bring you

breakfast in bed on Mother's Day, leave toaster waffles and orange juice readily available on the kitchen counter.

If you expect your teenagers to prepare dinner on that day, leave the freezer filled with frozen entrées, or better yet, leave the telephone number of your favorite takeout on every mirror in your house.

If you expect your grown children to invite you to their homes for dinner, forget it. On Mother's Day, there are no grown children. Everybody goes to Mom's!

So how, then, does my own mother get out of having us all for dinner at her house on Mother's Day?

I don't know; that's one secret she has never taught me.

8

CHRISTMAS DINNER

Christmas is coming! It's time for sending cards and singing carols, trimming the tree and wrapping the gifts, going to church and coming home to Santa Claus, all culminating in that delightful epicurean event: the traditional Christmas dinner.

Enjoy it, because it's on its way out.

Not Christmas. Christmas will be around as long as there is somebody to sell toys and ties and somebody else to expect the toys and exchange the ties. With any luck, even the Baby Jesus will continue celebrating birthdays. No, it's the traditional Christmas dinner I'm concerned about. What will happen to it when I, and other mothers of my generation, are dead and gone?

Do you realize that in this entire country there is not one person under the age of thirty who knows how to stuff a turkey? And why should they? Every Thanksgiving and Christmas they go to Mom's to eat!

This Christmas, as they do every year, our married children will come to our house for our traditional turkey-

and-all-the-trimmings dinner. In anticipation of the event, I will get up at dawn to stuff the turkey, then I will spend the morning setting the tables and peeling the potatoes and baking the pies and straining the cranberries because my newest daughter-in-law doesn't like them whole (and my daughter will say, "I never liked them whole either, but you never strained them for me," which is true, but I have no doubt her future mother-in-law will).

Just after noon our darlings will descend upon us, bearing gifts and diaper bags and pacifiers and other paraphernalia to see their offspring through the day. While my grandchildren play with their toys and entertain their grandpa, my children will wander out to the kitchen, where they will offer to "help," which means they will stand around the stove and pick at the turkey and taste the gravy and tell me how delicious my homemade stuffing smells and I must give them the recipe. (I have given it to them every holiday for six years; as far as I know, they have never used it.)

I don't really mind doing all the work on Christmas, but I do worry that I may be doing my children a disservice by never insisting that one or the other of them host the traditional family Christmas dinner.

Frankly, I wonder how any young matron can make her way in the world if she has never had to bake a twenty-pound turkey plus four pies, a potato casserole, and three dozen rolls, with only two ovens.

Can a woman consider herself truly sophisticated if she has never met the challenge of trying to set a table for twenty with only a dozen place settings of silverware? Or had to figure out how to whisk the salad plates off the table in time to rinse them for dessert? Or made the mind-boggling decision as to who should sit at the dining room table and who at the card tables in the living room and front hall?

And what father can succeed in business if he has never had to mix a batch of eggnog while simultaneously mashing a peck of potatoes? Or carved a turkey in such a manner as to disguise a thigh as white meat to appease an adolescent who "would *die* rather than eat dark meat!" Or cheerfully ate the turkey neck because that was all that was left by the time he served himself?

Isn't this all part of their education?

I was dwelling on this just this morning when my daughter-in-law called me and said that this year she wants to help me create the Christmas dinner.

"I'll come over very early," she said, "because I want to learn everything you do: stuffing the turkey, seasoning the vegetables, baking the pies, everything. I want to master the art of creating a truly traditional Christmas dinner."

"Well bless your heart," I said. "Of course I will teach you everything. And I must admit it is a relief to know that somebody will be carrying on the tradition of the family Christmas dinner."

"Oh, I'll be carrying it on all right," she said, "but not in the way you think. I'm going to start a takeout turkey business; I figure every holiday season I'll make a bundle! I just hope all you old-fashioned cooks won't resent me."

Resent her? Is she kidding? We'll be the ones who will make her rich!

9

WHEN I GROW UP...

Kids claim that they are being pressured at an earlier and earlier age to choose their college majors in preparation for their careers. Thus I guess I should not have been surprised when a group of second-graders from Loveland and Sunset Hills schools in Omaha, Nebraska, hesitated only moments before writing the following essays: "What I Want to Be When I Grow Up, and Why." My thanks to the teachers for sharing these gems of wisdom, and special thanks to the copy editors, typesetters, and proofreaders who took such pains to see that they came down the line exactly as written.

Lacey: I will be a docter. I will help people if they need help. I will do alergy shots x-rays testing their bodys. I will give them tempergers. I will do lots of stuff.

Troy: I will be a layer becas I like to be nice to people.

Chad: I will be a vet because I like aimels and if one of them are hrrt I take caer of them.

Ryan: I woled like to be a fire man. If I can not be a fireman I woled like to work for Union Pacific becas it woled be fun bving a fireman. the rseine I woled like to work for UP is my dad works for UP and I like tranes.

Charles: I am gong to be a Pilot. Becaus I thingk it would be fun flying. I could see montan tops and snow would fly at the wincheeld.

Nicole: I want to be a gymnest because I *love* doing gymnastekes. (And that *is* the truth!) My favorite is cartwheels!

Seth: I want to be a poter. Because I like to work with clay. I wuld make pots and bols and either things.

Theodore: I would whant to be a hospell docter besces my frends dad is a hospoll docter and he things its fun besces he wokes in the srger room.

Michael: I will be a Army. I want to be a Army because I can run and ride a jeep and ride on a jet.

Marilyn: I would like to be a teacher because I thinh it is a nice job and I like my teachers. I think my teachers are the best ones I evee will have.

Philip: I would like to be a sailer. Because I like to sail and I like to fish and fix botes.

Jimmy: It would be fun to be a doctor because you help people and make them feel better. And the time you make them feel better youll get lots and lots of Money Money! Money! Money! And then the sick people go in peace.

Kim: I want to be a teacher because my mom is a teacher and also I want a big desk.

Rachel: I want to be a vet because I like to tack care of animls.

Courtney: I want to be an arttist. I like to draw. I like to paint to. I like to cut and paste to.

Brett: I want to be a photeographer and tack pitcers of anmals.

Janice: I want to be a baby setter. because I love kid's and I wold like to hold her.

Matt: I want to be a rockstar. Becus I like misic and to play drums.

Jason: Im gong to be a macanik. Becus I like to get my hand durte and rebelde car bratrs. Well I need to get a toole box. I mite make a plase called Jason's macaniks.

Saamant: It would be iterestig to be a firefiter. I like to put out fires and I like to work.

Megan: I want to be a veterinarinarian. Because I love animals and they also get a lot of mony. And they are also fun to play with.

Kendra: I want to be a hairstyler because I like to do peoples hair. I like the way my hair is. I no it will take lots of practis but Im loking froword to it.

Jennifer: Im going to be a police officer because officers helpes the people. I think officers get a lot uv mone.

Will: I will work at the fish bole. They have over 1000 fish and soltwater aquawums and raglry. I want to work thir because I think fish are aspeshlee interresting.

Dionna: I want to be a movie stair. Becauise I think Im very pretty. I think Ill be a good movie stair becauise I think Im a good atrris.

Jeremy: Im going to be a scientist because I want to make weird potions and find out interesting things and take animals apart and study the inside of them.

Chris: I want to be an artest because I'm a good artest now. My favret way to drow is to put animles or pepol in it.

John: I want to be a electrishan because I would have a bigjob and fix lights.

Larry: I will be a nasternot because I like to explor it would be very fun training.

David: Time passes . . . years into the fuecher. Ill have three children. With a doctors job. And my mony? Well I wont have much more than my parents. The resen wiy I fell that way is becouse I have a hapy life with the my famly dus have. And docters get anogh mony to make me and my famly happy.

Lauren: I will be a aertist because it souns fun and think I coud do the job well. I would drow things like rainbows.

Joy: I want to be a teacher because I like to write I would also like to be an artist because my ant is a artist.

Cherie: I want to be a nurse because I like to help people to get better and I want to help as many people as I can to stay alive.

Allison: I want to be a preskool teacher because I love children. Its fun being a kid.

Josh: I want to be a veternarin becuase I want to take care of bunnys.

Cindy: I want to be a teacher because you can met lots of children when you or a teacher.

Jennifer: I want to be a vet becas I like anamles and becas Im nice to anamles and becas anamles like me.

Missy: I want to be a vetineren becuse I love anmoles one resen is they are quite. Anther resen is they are playful.

Maggie: When I grow up I won to be a perfeshenal artst because I like to draw color and paint. sometimes it is heard to stay in the lines but I try.

Jason: I want to work at chanl 7. It would be fun because you get to see whats going on and I like bing on tv.

Ann: I think it would be nice to be a techer and be with childrn and make things and hang them up for people to see and be able to look up to them.

George: I want to be a doctor because I want to help people so they dont get sick and help them get well when there are sick and to get more money. Also I want to be a football player.

Allison: I want to be a Vetanarein. For dog and cats. I will give them shos to help them.

Carly: I will be an artest because I drow good.

Jenni: I will be a dansr. I go to dans class and dans a lot.

Scott: I want to be a doctor. Because it would be neet!

T.W.: I want to be a cowboy becos my dad is a cowboy becos horses are nice.

Mark: I wood like to be a farmer because I like pigs and tracktors.

Terri: I think I will be a tense star and play tense on tv or maybe I will be a gofer.

10

I NEVER PROMISED YOU
A CLEAN KITCHEN

"Who left these dirty dishes in the sink?" asked my husband this morning, as he has asked each and every morning since the first of our ten children was weaned to peanut butter, and I answered, as I have each and every morning for lo these many years, "Nobody; that sink came with predirtied dishes."

Of course I could have told him what he already knew: that one or more of our children had a midnight snack, but such a reminder just makes him upset with the kids, or worse, upset with me for not being upset with the kids.

"What are you going to do about this?" he asked, as he always does, and I promised, as I always do, that I would seek out the culprit or culprits and give them a sound scolding.

I don't know why he gets so upset. Frankly, I am so grateful that our kids have outgrown the dirty-dishes-under-the-bed stage, I can't get too appalled about dirty dishes in the sink.

Don't ask me why children in their upper teens cannot rinse a plate and put it in an easily accessible dishwasher. I don't know why; I doubt if they know why. This is simply one of life's little mysteries that parents must learn to accept, and never try to solve.

As Eliot's Prüfrock measured out his life in coffee spoons, mothers measure out their lives in dirty dishes. No matter how many times a day we clean up the kitchen, dirty dishes continue to sprout around us, unbidden, unwanted, and unclaimed.

'Who had the bowl of cereal?" I will ask when I walk into the kitchen I left spotless fifteen minutes before. Nobody answers.

"Who left this coffee cup on the counter by the telephone?" Nobody did.

"Where did this pizza carton come from?" (As they can't find the dishwasher, neither can they locate the wastebasket.) Nobody knows.

We've lived with Nobody for years.

But not always. When the kids were little, I had no trouble finding a culprit, for a younger child was always eager to get an older sibling in trouble.

"John did it!" . . . "Mike ate it!" . . . "Jim took it!" a younger child would claim, not so much to see justice done as to watch the ax fall. (I'm surprised the five oldest let the five youngest live to grow up.)

Sometimes a simple clue would lead me to the culprit. It wasn't difficult to discern just who was responsible for the sour-smelling ice cream dish when said dish was discovered under Danny's bed. Nor could Peggy proclaim ignorance of the jelly donut plate, since the plate was on the floor by her bed and the jelly was dried on her pillow.

However, as the children grew older, they became

more devious. After sneaking a snack to their bedroom and devouring same, they would deposit the dirty dishes in somebody else's bedroom . . . a glass here, a plate there, and to make the game more interesting, a mug, perhaps, on the stairway landing.

Thus I would be frustrated in my sleuthing, and often mete out unjust punishment, though as my friend Joyce says, "Is such punishment ever unjust? If he isn't guilty this time, he probably was last time, when somebody else got blamed." Wise mother, Joyce.

It wasn't the messy bedrooms that got to me so much as the empty kitchen cabinets. Every time I would reach for a glass (of which we had dozens), I would clutch empty air. None were there. Cups would disappear as fast as I would place them on the shelf. Cereal bowls became extinct. My mother used to glance into my kitchen cabinets and wonder where I kept my dishes. How could I tell her they were moldering under the beds of her precious, perfect grandchildren?

As our children reach college age, however, a miracle occurs. They shed their pigsty personalities, and bedrooms I couldn't have climbed through yesteryear become so neat I dare not place clean laundry on a bed, or toss a notebook on a desk, lest I hear cries of "Who messed up my room?" (Hang in there, parents, it *does* happen.)

Their neatness, unfortunately, does not extend to the kitchen, where the cups and mugs that used to be left under their beds are now left stacked in the sink, though nobody ever seems to recall placing them there.

I know that tomorrow we shall go through the same routine again, with my husband claiming that the dirty dishes were left in the sink for the sole purpose of driving him crazy, and me assuring him that I will do something about it.

And I will. I will speak firmly, and harshly, to Nobody.

11

BLOOMINGDALE'S BOARDING HOUSE

The Bureau of the Census reports that in the past decade the number of young adults opting to live with their parents until marriage has increased dramatically.

I knew that.

The report indicated that because people are now taking longer to get through college (I knew that too) or have chosen careers which are not lucrative enough to allow them a standard of living they consider "appropriate" (the Aga Khan should live so well), these "otherwise independent, mature adults are forced to live with their parents." (Why do I feel that should read the other way around?)

I did not contribute statistics for that report, but I could have. We currently have so many "otherwise independent, mature adults" living at our house the neighbors are beginning to think we run a hotel. (They're being kind; it's actually more of an open-door mission.)

I am referring only to our out-of-college, gainfully employed offspring. I am perfectly willing to give house-room and even financial support to those of our children who are still in college, though we are considering a seven-year limit for sophomores. However, I do think the "otherwise independents" should be on their own, yet they take the very mention of such a move as an insult. ("But this is my home! Where would I go? You don't love me!")

I can't understand them. When I was their age I couldn't wait to get my own place. The ink was hardly dry on my college diploma before I had signed a lease on a tiny, non-air-conditioned, unfurnished apartment. My parents thought I was crazy. Why would I want to trade my beautiful, comfortable home—complete with designer-decorated bedroom, complimentary meals, parent-paid clothes, and round-the-clock maid service (my mother) —for an overcrowded apartment (I shared expenses, as well as the one bedroom, with two other girls), skipped lunches, bargain basement clothes, dishpan hands, and housemaid's knee? Why would I want to live like that? (Why? My God, I can't remember! Maybe I *was* crazy!)

If my kids had my mother for a mother, I could understand why they would want to live at home forever, but they don't. They don't even have me for a mother, because the moment I see one of my adult children walk into the house with that first full-time paycheck, I turn into a landlady. I not only expect them to pay room and board, I also insist that they pay for their own clothes, provide their own transportation (that may have been a mistake; the city just notified me we're not zoned for a used car lot), keep a reasonable curfew, reimburse me for long distance telephone calls, and do a proportionate share of the housework (keep in mind there are seven of them; how much can "proportionate" be?)

The only thing I do for them is cook, though lately they have been complaining that all I ever prepare for dinner anymore is a note stating: "Your father and I are eating out; fend for yourselves." Even that wouldn't bother them, they say, if they could ever find anything in the refrigerator other than their father's photographic film, my migraine medicine, and an occasional package of lunch meat with a memo from a sibling: "I bought this with my own money. Touch it and you're dead."

I truly can't understand why they continue to live here. If I was their age, I'd move out in a minute. Yet they seem perfectly content. What did I do wrong?

That census report also mentioned the fact that while young single adults are choosing to live at home with their parents, middle-aged married couples are opting to give up their home for an apartment or condominium.

Guess why.

Part Two

BACK TO THE BASICS ...
OR FORWARD?

12

THERE ARE NO ATHEISTS
IN ALGEBRA CLASS

Sometimes I think we Americans just like to argue.

When the amendment for prayer in the public schools came before Congress, every American with a mouth had something to say about it, either pro or con. Nobody was neutral. Everybody had an opinion, and everybody voiced it, loudly and clearly, though sometimes incomprehensibly, such as the fellow who proclaimed, "I am an atheist, my wife is an atheist, and by God, my kids are going to be atheists!"

I admit that I am for some form of prayer in the schools, not only because I think kids have a right to learn about God and the efficacy of prayer, but also because I think teachers need all the heavenly help they can get.

It tickles me that some of the more radical critics object to such "prayers" as the reading of a beautiful psalm, or a simple "God bless us today." (I assume it's no longer permissible for kids to say, "May the Force be with you!") They call that *praying?* They should have gone to school with me!

I went to a convent school where we opened every school day with a prayer to the Sacred Heart, began each class with an invocation to the Holy Ghost (now called the Holy Spirit, but I like to brag that I know Him so well I can call Him by His first name), went out to recess invoking the protection of our guardian angels, paused at noon to say the Angelus (not to mention grace before and after lunch), and concluded our school day with a prayer to St. Madeleine Sophie. This did not count "feast days," on which, along with the aforementioned prayers, we attended Holy Mass, recited the Litany of the Blessed Mother, said the Rosary, or made the Stations of the Cross (depending on the holy day), and ended the day with the Benediction of the Most Blessed Sacrament.

Now *that* was *prayer*.

So what's all the fuss about a little God-talk? Or even God-think?

While the prayer amendment did not pass, there is still talk of having a "moment of silence" during the school day, and we ever-opinionated, love-to-argue Americans are back to our bickering.

I find it hard to believe that any parent would protest a moment of silence in the classroom. (I find it harder to believe that any teacher could *get* a moment of silence in the classroom.) The protest, of course, is not against the moment of silence per se, but rather what that moment of silence implies: that the students will feel compelled to "think" prayers.

The critics can put their minds at rest. Even if we get that moment of silence, I, as a mother of ten children and former teacher of many more, can practically guarantee that if students (of any age) are forced to keep silent for seconds, the last thing they'll conjure up is a prayer.

Especially in junior high. A seventh-, eighth-, or ninth-grade boy, on being told he must meditate for a moment, will surely dwell on those things which are uppermost in his mind: football, basketball, baseball, or track, depending on the season.

A junior high girl likewise will dwell on those things which are uppermost in her mind in every season: junior high boys.

In the middle grades, meditation may be more meaningful. A ten-year-old boy can compound a lot of thinking into sixty seconds: How can a teacher be so ugly? How can I get out of today's piano lesson? How far can I spit? A ten-year-old girl, on the other hand, may be absorbed with only one thought: Why is everybody staring at me?

As far as the primary children are concerned, the thoughts will be the same for both genders. Forced to stand, or even sit still, for sixty seconds, a six-year-old will only wonder: How can one minute last so long?

And, of course, in high school there would be no problem. To teenagers, a moment of silence would not only be welcome, but also well spent. They would simply catch up on their sleep.

Instead of arguing over what students might be thinking during a moment of silence in the classroom, it seems to me it would be more beneficial to argue over why there aren't more moments of silence in the schools.

Whatever the arguments, no one will ever be successful in banning prayer in the schools. Whether it's verbally, silently, in unison, or alone, if there is an algebra exam that day, or a basketball tournament that night, the students involved are going to *pray*.

13

A SURE CURE FOR CHEATING

University administrators, alarmed over the amount of cheating that is taking place on college campuses, have come up with a unique form of punishment which they hope will act as a deterrent. Students caught cheating are still getting the expected F and the damning notation on the permanent record cards indicating that on one occasion, at least, this kid was a no-goodnick, but they are also being "sentenced" to a specific and nonpaid job on campus.

For example, at the University of California at Berkeley, a junior caught plagiarizing a sociology paper was required to work forty hours in the library, while at the University of Oregon, a freshman who neglected to mention the fact that his English papers had originated elsewhere was sentenced to fifteen hours of janitorial work in the student union.

This is the wrong way to go, fellas; take it from one who knows.

As a mother of eight college students (of course only six of them are in college at the present time), I can tell you that sending a college kid to the student union is like sending a ten-year-old to his room (where he has a radio, stereo, electronic games, TV, and maybe even his own phone); there is too much distraction to get any work done. And certainly not in fifteen hours! I've been in student unions, and believe me, in fifteen hours one couldn't even get all the straws picked up around the soda fountain.

And for God's sake, keep those cheaters out of the library! Do you have any idea how much damage can be done to the Dewey decimal system in forty hours? And what cheater could resist the opportunity to shuffle the stacks and thereby frustrate the goody-goody scholars who frequent the place? No, don't send them to the library.

In fact, it might be better to forget the cure and concentrate on the cause. Why do kids cheat?

Now it may be true that a few serious-minded students cheat because they are overextended and fold under pressure, but surely most cheaters cheat because they think it's easier than work.

Wrong. Cheating involves an enormous effort and a great deal of time. Some cheaters have been known to spend twenty hours browsing through books searching for one passable plagiarism when, in fact, the entire paper could have been whipped off originally in less time than it takes to eat lunch. Why doesn't anybody explain this to the little stupies?

Others cheat because they want a good grade, or at least a passing grade, so they steal somebody else's stuff.

Stupid, stupid, stupid. What makes them think that somebody else's stuff will please the prof?

Authors are familiar with the legendary story of the writer who, sick of repeated rejections, copied a bestselling novel and sent it off to a publisher, only to have it rejected. Are professors any more predictable than publishers? Steal an essay from Emerson, and chances are your teacher will hate Emerson. (Very good chances, in fact; so if you must steal, go to Thoreau. Everybody likes Thoreau.)

Few cheaters steal from the classics; most go the more traditional route of buying an A paper from an older student. This is even a greater risk, for whatever they say about "absentminded" professors, they are never so absentminded that they forget an A paper written during their own tenure.

Furthermore, faculty members tend to be fickle. Yesterday's jewel may be today's junk.

I realize that plagiarists must be punished, and as one who has been associated with various colleges and universities for two generations, I offer the following "cure."

Instead of sentencing cheaters to work on campus, make them eat on campus, every single meal for at least a semester.

The food may be delicious, but the kids will still swear they are suffering.

14

WHY DON'T THEY JUST GO
TO THE LIBRARY?

Here we go again.

College kids all over the country are rebelling, à la their predecessors of the sixties, though as one professor said, "The student protestors of the sixties were pacifists; their idea of a protest was to sit on the fioor of the dean's office and refuse to move until the dean got so tired of climbing over unwashed bodies he capitulated to their demands. These kids today scream and shout and pound our desks and demand immediate action!"

The "action" the students want is a retraction of "new" dormitory rules forbidding (1) late-night visitation from members of the opposite sex and, (2) the drinking of alcoholic beverages in the dorm rooms.

Technically, drinking has always been forbidden on most college campuses, but dorm rooms, like foreign embassies, were acknowledged to be the private domain of the occupant and off-limits to such "unfriendlies" as dorm supervisors, campus police, university personnel, and, presumably, parents.

It is understandable, therefore, why dorm rooms became the most popular party sites on campus, and equally understandable why such events would draw members of the opposite sex.

Where the kids blew it was in getting loud. If they had kept everything quiet they could have stayed bombed all year. But as kids will, they enhanced their drinking with singing and shouting, often into the wee hours of the morning.

As the noise got louder and the hours got later, and the swinging seventies evolved into the sensible eighties, some serious-minded students began to complain that they could neither study nor sleep nor even change their clothes for lack of privacy. One sophomore refused to make her housing payment on the grounds that she hadn't been able to get into her room for five weeks; a premed student blamed his poor grades on his noisy dorm-mates, while his sister, who lived in an all-girl dorm, argued, "It's not the noise I mind, it's the danger of having all these drunks around every might! Somebody could get hurt!" (They should have listened to her. Four days later she was knocked down and badly bruised, though it has not yet been proven that the two guys riding their bicycles through the eighth-floor shower room had actually been drinking.)

Because of student complaints, not to mention the rising cost of repairs, university officials have begun to crack down on the old rules and establish new ones.

The students, of course, are rebelling, and while they are looking to the students of the sixties for ideas and inspiration, I attest they have the wrong decade. They should be looking to college students of the fifties. The students of the sixties angrily, and often ineffectively, protested rules; the kids in the fifties just cheerfully broke them.

I was in college in the fifties, and we had rules that were ridiculous. Not only was late-night visiting from boys forbidden, *any* visiting from males was forbidden. (On rare occasions, if a student was deathly ill, a doctor might be allowed to visit her, but he could only come as far as the infirmary, and even then he was "chaperoned" by two nuns and a nurse.)

As for alcoholic beverages, bringing beer or liquor into the dorm was tantamount to breaking all ten of the commandments, which the nuns were sure we would do anyway if we let liquor pass our lips. Actually, few of us had ever tasted the stuff; we didn't need the "lift" or the "thrill"; we got that simply by breaking rules.

Can you imagine the thrill of sneaking fraternity men into a convent college dorm where every door had two bolts, a watchdog, and a security guard who was *armed?* Some of the guys dressed in drag to sneak into our forbidden domain; others tried to pass themselves off as plumbers or repairmen or somebody's brother, but that seldom worked. What nun would believe that a Phi Delt would spend Saturday night visiting his sister?

The more daring sneaked up the fire escape, which was really stupid, as it was one of those rickety metal outdoor stairways that was so ancient it had a student-inscribed sign saying: IN CASE OF FIRE, PROCEED AT YOUR OWN RISK.

Whatever, however, it was always possible for enterprising college men to invade our inner sanctum, though once there they seldom stayed around, because what place is duller than a convent girls' dormitory?

Even more fun than breaking in, however, was the

challenge of breaking out. As our "hours" were ridiculous (9 P.M. on weeknights, 12:30 A.M. on weekends), those of us who were enjoying a really swinging party had to check in at curfew and then figure out how to sneak out again.

Sneaking out was even harder than sneaking in, because while one security guard was watching out for the boys, ninety-nine nuns had their eyes on us. I went to parties I didn't even care about just for the fun of "breaking out."

Which explains why we never bothered to sneak liquor into the dorms. Who wanted to party in a dormitory? We had better places to do our partying, the most popular place being The Library. (No, not the library, The Library. The Library was a brilliantly named off-campus bar where the students loved to congregate because when they checked out of or into the dorm they could truthfully say they were going to, or had been at, The Library. An added benefit was the fact that phoning parents could be told, "Your daughter? Oh, she's at The Library; been there every night this week!" I wonder if there are any more Library bars, since their patrons became parents!)

Breaking rules was half the fun of college life in the fifties. I'm not surprised today's college students drink in their dorms; they don't have anything better to do!

15

THE *DIVINE COMEDY*—REVISED

Last night I dreamt I died and went to purgatory.

The dream was inspired, I have no doubt, by the job I had tackled that day. My collegiate son Dan had written a paper on Dante's *Divine Comedy*, or more specifically, on the *Purgatorio*, and because the paper was due yesterday and he still had three more to write, I agreed to type it for him. It was not a long paper, but by the time I had deciphered his notes, figured out where to put the paragraphs (when he talks he doesn't stop to breathe, so I suppose it is natural that when he writes he wouldn't bother to indent), and corrected his spelling and grammar, I had devoted an entire day to Dan and Dante.

I finished the paper at midnight, fell into bed exhausted, and almost immediately found myself in Dante's purgatory.

It was almost exactly as Dante describes it: Vergil to greet me, and a spiral staircase ascending through the seven circles, but the sinners were not the same.

"That's because the sins aren't the same," said Vergil

with a sigh. "If we opened this place up to everybody who was lazy or lustful, we couldn't begin to get everybody in. But I think you'll be interested in seeing who we do have here."

I was interested, but not surprised.

In one of the hottest circles, I saw hundreds of rock musicians (who had, on earth, deafened millions with their "music") standing before huge amplifiers, holding their ears and grimacing as the music of Bach, Benny Goodman, Mozart, and Mancini played repeatedly throughout the circle.

"But that's no punishment!" I said as the music changed to Fred Waring and the Pennsylvanians.

"It is to them," said Vergil. "This isn't the worst though; over there in the corner you'll see those who sang obscene lyrics, or allowed subliminal messages on their albums. They have to listen to Kate Smith."

In the next circle I saw a group of people frantically trying to package items in boxes that were too small, using string that was too short, and labels that wouldn't stick.

"Who are they?" I asked as a half-wrapped package was hurled across the circle in frustration.

"Mail-order con artists," said Vergil. "Those are the guys who kept sending out unordered merchandise to people who felt obligated to box them up and send them back, if only to put an end to the ceaseless billing."

In the next circle, there were more people wrapping packages, but this circle was freezing cold.

"Why is it so cold in here?" I asked. "I thought purgatory was supposed to be hot?"

"Not this circle," said Vergil. "It wouldn't be punishment enough for these guys. They're pornographers who circulated obscene pictures and paraphernalia; you'll notice we make them work in the nude. We thought that was a nice touch."

The next circle was filled with well-dressed gentlemen all sitting in chairs, reading dog-eared magazines, and looking at their watches.

"This is one of our most popular circles," said Vergil. "These are all doctors."

"Doctors?" I asked. "But what are they doing?"

"Waiting," explained Vergil with a wicked grin. "Just waiting. Their patients promised to be in at two, but of course they'll be late. I must admit I love to visit this circle. I had a bad back when I was alive, you know."

We could hardly open the door of the next circle, it was so filled with dirty laundry. I was surprised to see only three people there, all teenagers frantically trying to do huge loads of laundry as even more dirty clothes piled up around them.

"These are the kids who would use fifty gallons of water to wash one pair of jeans, then pull a load of wet clothes out of the dryer onto the floor in order to dry those jeans. They must spend their entire time here doing laundry."

"I can understand that," I said, "but why so few of them; I count only three, and almost all teenagers are guilty of that sin."

"Ah, yes," he said, "but many of those grew up to be parents, and served their purgatory on earth."

I was absolutely astounded when I climbed to the next circle and found it filled with clergymen, all standing at pulpits.

"Surely clergymen don't have to go to purgatory!" I exclaimed.

"Not for long," said Vergil. "As soon as each one

learns to cut his sermon to ten minutes, he gets to go to heaven."

We then reached the top circle, and Vergil said:

"This circle is not necessarily for sinners, but for those who were just stupid. This is where *you* will be."

"Me?" I asked. "I don't belong here; there must be some mistake."

"I don't think so," said Vergil. "Didn't you just spend ten hours typing a term paper for a kid who knows how to type, rewriting what he was too lazy to compose himself, thereby earning him a grade he doesn't deserve? What would you call that?"

"Stupid," I admitted as I humbly entered the Stupidity Circle. "How long will I be here?"

"I have no idea," he said, "because to be honest with you, I have never seen a mother come out."

"You haven't?" I asked in horror.

"No," he said. "Every time I send one in here, just as soon as God finds out about it he sends St. Peter down to sneak her out the back door and up to heaven. You're almost home free!"

What a helluva time to wake up.

16

BACK TO THE BASICS ...
OR FORWARD?

No one is more concerned than I about the alleged illiteracy among Americans today, but I must take issue with those critics who want our children taught "the basic education of yesteryear" so they can do "such simple tasks as filling out an income tax form and balancing a checking account."

I hate to admit to such an ancient age, but I am a product of "yesterday's basics." We not only learned "reading, 'riting and 'rithmetic" (though obviously not spelling), but we also took algebra until we *understood* it; we memorized Shakespeare, Tennyson, T. S. Eliot, and G. B. Shaw; we studied our world history in three languages (English, Latin, French and/or Spanish), learned the difference between a cappella and a capriccio and between Rembrandt and Renoir, and we were introduced to such a wide variety of philosophers we were the first to understand and appreciate Pogo, Peanuts, and Doonesbury.

What we did not learn to do was fill out a tax return or balance a checkbook.

Teaching those talents today would be a waste of time, however, because (a) by the time we figure out one tax form it is replaced by another, more complicated one and, (b) money gets spent so fast these days it doesn't have time to go through a checking account.

There *are* a few subjects about which we could all be made more literate, however, and I name here a few:

The telephone bill. The new telephone system has been in effect for over a year now and to my knowledge not one phone owner can figure out his bill. It's true that the bill lists a number to be called for "information and assistance" but it doesn't help to call it because it's always busy. (And for heaven's sake, don't try to "verify" that busy, or you'll add another page of code on your next bill.)

Credit card statements. Assuming that you are affluent enough to get a credit card, and stupid enough to use one, it is unlikely that you have the necessary know-how to interpret your monthly statement. Oh sure, you may understand about "average daily balances," "old purchases," "current purchases," "credit limit," "billing cycle," and the difference between "deferred finance charges," "billed finance charges," and just plain "finance charges," but have you ever been able to figure out why it is that no matter when you get around to paying that bill, the "payment due date" is always past?

Easy-to-assemble instructions. I long ago concluded that this term means that the *instructions* are easy to assemble, not the merchandise. (Page 5 follows page 4, which follows page 3, etc., etc.) Nowadays even that is no longer true, as the instructions are in Japanese or Korean, and so numbered. Even in the days when such instructions were in English we couldn't interpret them because whatever the merchandise, the instructions were for the other model. (At least we knew what was missing.)

Road maps. Is there, or has there ever been, a road map that was published *after* the highway you're on was completed?

Report cards. Last semester my son's report card read: "P, P, W, S, N, and I." Whatever happened to "A, B, C, D, F"? And when did "Conduct" become "Citizenship"? Does this mean that if he doesn't shape up he'll be deported? (To where? Who'd have him?)

Traffic tickets. It's not the incomprehensibility of traffic tickets that makes them impossible to read; it's the illegibility. (But for God's sake don't suggest better carbons, or they'll raise our taxes again.)

Utility meters. Remember the good old days when a bright young man would knock on your kitchen door once a month and ask permission to read your meters? Now we are expected to read our own meters, which means we must understand such things as therms and BTU's and watts and kilowatts. I was crawling behind the furnace last week trying to read our meters when my youngest son came downstairs and offered to help. He took a quick glance at the meters, rattled off the secret code, and quickly drew a diagram for me to send to the utility company.

Don't tell me today's young people are illiterate. This kid cannot only read meters, he can also find a number in the telephone book (even one listed under "U.S. Government"!), fill out warranty cards and registration forms, talk computerese, understand the metric system, find the price in a six-page junk mail brochure, remember the toll-free number rattled off by television announcers, and even read my mind when I am furious with him and think unspoken swear words.

But I'm still smarter than he is. I swear in Latin.

17

WATCH YOUR LANGUAGE!

"I zeenck you are expecting too much of your scheeldren," said my French houseguest, Michelle, as she helped me set the table for a luncheon I was giving in her honor.

"What do you mean?" I asked, and she replied:

"Zjust now, you told zem to go 'peeck up' zee living room. How can anyone 'peeck up' a room? And even eef zay could, why would you want zem to? And where would zay put eet? Why do you say zees 'peeck up'?"

I explained to her that "picking up" a room meant "to straighten" it.

"Straighten eet?" she asked. "Why? Eez eet crooked?"

"Not crooked," I said. "Messy. I want them to pick up their books and record albums or whatever, and put them away."

"You have a funny way of saying zat," she said. "Americans, I zeenck, have a funny way of saying many zeengs."

"Like what?" I asked her as we set a water goblet at each place.

"Like what we are doing now," said Michelle. "You

say we are 'setteeng' zee table. But you see zee table eet ees already setting. We are zjust putteeng zings on eet."

She was right, of course. The American language (the British will no longer allow us to refer to it as English) is complicated, confusing, and in many cases senseless. Not only do we have phonetic inconsistencies ("rough," "bough," "thought," and "through" don't even rhyme, for heaven's sake), but we also goof up our grammar. (If "reform" means "to change a form," why doesn't "repeat" mean "to change a peat"?) We also use phrases which, if taken literally, don't make any sense. Such as:

Tell time. (What do we tell it? "Slow down"? "Hurry up"? "You stupid clock, you can't be right?")

Beat the clock. (This has no relation to what you are tempted to do when the darn clock *is* right.)

Simmer down. (Impossible. You can "heat up" or "cool down," but if you "simmer" you can't go anyplace.)

Hit the ceiling. (What you do if you simmer up.)

Pass the buck. (Nobody in their right mind would pass a buck. Bucks you hang on to; it's problems you pass.)

Shake a leg. (Why does this mean "hurry up" and not "hurry down"? And if you stop to shake your leg, how can you hurry anyplace?)

Steal a glance. (Oddly enough, this is correct. The "glance" is what you get, not what you give.)

Do the dishes. (After a big dinner party, I'm tempted to "do them in!")

Take a nap. (To where? If you "take a nap" why don't you "take a sleep"? Or "go to nap"? And wherever did they get the word "nap"?)

Grease a palm. (Money is much more effective.)

Watch your language. (Forget "watch"; *listen!*)

Cut it out. (And paste it in your scrapbook?)

Mind your mother. (Before she loses hers.)

Fix dinner. (Only if it's broken.)

Make your bed. (Make it *what?* Behave?)

Pay attention. (Why? What did attention ever do for you?)

Stand pat. (Only makes sense if you are speaking to Patrick or Patricia.)

Let up. (If "let *up*" means "to slow down," what does "let *down*" mean?)

Let down. (How she feels when he lets up?)

Pass out. (Worse than passing in, but better than passing on!)

Beside oneself. (One can be "ahead of oneself," but not "behind oneself," which is ridiculous because that's where most of us are, which explains why we're so often "beside ourselves.")

Dressing down. (Means "scolding," not the opposite of "dressing up.")

Dressing up. (That which my French friend, Michelle, has been afraid to do ever since somebody told her she was dressed up "fit to kill.")

"Eet ees amazing," said Michelle after our guests had gone, "your language, eet ees so confusing, yet even zee leetlest scheeldren seem to comprehend. Zee leetle boy who was here, hees *grand'mère* told heem to 'seet down' and his *maman* told him to 'seet up' and he deed not even say, 'How can I do boz at zee same time?'"

Of course he didn't. That boy knew very well that if he smarted off to his mother, she would whale the daylights out of him later.

18

"MY DEAR SIMON..."

"Top Secret! Private! Confidential!"

Have you ever wondered why books that are dreadfully dull often sell like hotcakes, while books that are exciting and well written languish on the remainder tables? (I know you're wondering about "Top Secret! etc." Be patient; I'll get to that.)

I was browsing in a bookstore recently, and I became intrigued watching the customers as they picked up one book and then another, trying to find something to their liking.

What do readers look for in a book? An interesting subject? A favorite author? An intriguing style? Dirty pictures? Is there one single factor that prompts a reader to buy one book and not another?

I contend that there is a secret ingredient that hooks a reader, but it is not the subject, title, author, or pictures. It's the first line of the book.

I don't mean the first line of the foreword, prologue, or introduction, because I never read those (does anybody?) except perhaps one that has been guest-written for the author by a celebrity, in which case that is the only part of the book I do read, usually while I'm standing in the bookstore deciding not to buy the book. (Because if it's any good, why did they need a celebrity to "introduce" it?)

No, I am referring to the first line of the first chapter, which any true book lover will read before he buys a book or even checks it out of a library. If that first line isn't a grabber, forget it.

Editors and authors may disagree with me about that, but let's be honest. Would *you* buy a book that begins: "The dusty road stretched interminably into the distance where barren hills rose into the leaden sky and darkened clouds hung heavily over the dreary landscape"? Bored already, aren't you?

The first line of any book must be a real grabber, and I am convinced that the most popular first line is:

"She was naked."

Show me a man who can read that line and put down the book and I'll show you a man whose wife is reading over his shoulder. In fact, I defy anybody to read that line and not the next, though I admit the next better quickly describe "naked" as "young, voluptuous, and seductive" lest the reader, who all too often tends to relate to real life, think "old, wrinkled, and shivering." The third line might even have whoever is naked standing at a window, smoking a cigarette, and watching the sunrise, thus leaving no doubt in the reader's mind just why she is naked, what she has been doing, and for how long.

Incidentally, she has to be "naked," not "nude." "Nude" has been so overused it's no longer noteworthy. "Naked," on the other hand, went out with a generation that never even *thought* naked, let alone stood at a window in such a state, so "naked" is still enough of a no-no to rate first-line status.

Another sure-fire first line is "He was dead." This line is more effective if it stands alone, as in:

"He was dead."

New paragraph. This leads the reader to believe that "he" is really *somebody* (or *was* really somebody, if you must be technical) and that the reason for as well as the method of his demise provides a tale worth telling.

It should be noted that in these first lines the magnetism will be lost if the genders are interchanged.

"He was naked" won't work unless he is also dead, in which case it's better to go with dead and forget naked.

And "she was dead" won't work even if she is also naked, and forget that flashback foolishness. Who cares if she used to be gorgeous and voluptuous; the readers all know that *now* she's *dead*.

Another favorite first line is:

"The phone was ringing insistently as she fumbled with her key, trying to unlock her apartment door."

Who among us can let a ringing phone go unanswered? (My husband claims that he never feels compelled to answer the phone. This is true. What he is compelled to do is yell, "Isn't anybody going to answer that damn thing?")

If there is anything more compelling than a ringing phone, it is a phone ringing on the other side of a door we can't get unlocked. We are all going to read through that first chapter, if only to find out who is calling, and God help the author if the phone stops ringing before it gets answered. (Which happens all too often because some authors are *sadistic*.)

Personally, my favorite first line is the salutation of a letter. I can't even not read a letter addressed to "Dear Occupant"; I certainly can't refrain from reading one addressed to "My Dear Simon . . ." (Why Simon? Think about it. Of all the novels you've read, have you ever come across a Simon who wasn't handsome, sexy, mysterious, incredibly attractive, and deliciously dangerous? Of course we're going to peek at his correspondence!)

The all-time favorite first line, however, is:

"The following is top secret, private, and confidential; for authorized eyes only!"

There isn't a reader around who doesn't believe his eyes aren't authorized.

19

ON USING EUPHEMISMS

Mea culpa.

I am guilty, but while I admit the fault, I argue the theory that it is one.

The fault, according to wordsmith James J. (Jack) Kilpatrick, is my excessive use of euphemisms. (I should explain that Mr. Kilpatrick wasn't picking on me personally; he is out to get all of us who speak euphemistically. God knows how he puts up with his pal Bill Buckley.)

I must admit that until I read Jack Kilpatrick's wonderful and witty book *The Writer's Art*, I wasn't even sure what a euphemism was. (Euphemism *is?* Since reading that book, I am no longer sure what *anything* is. I haven't been so insecure since Edwin Newman told me I wasn't speaking strictly.)

A euphemism (for you out there who won't admit that you don't know what it means, either) is a mild, agreeable word used as a substitute for a coarser or more offensive one. ("Filling out" for "getting fat"; "maturing" for "aging"; "sleeping with" for . . . well, you get the idea.)

Mr. Kilpatrick claims that all too often euphemisms are artificial or even deceptive and really should be avoided whenever possible. While I agree that some euphemisms are ridiculous ("low-income status" instead of just plain "poor," "therapeutic misadventure" for "medical malpractice," "domestic engineer" for me; this is supposed to sound better than "housewife"?) I argue that in many instances a euphemism is preferable to the original word or phrase, and therefore should be permissible, or maybe even mandatory, assuming, of course, that it is not too obtuse.

For example, in my book *I Should Have Seen It Coming When the Rabbit Died*, I use the phrase "poopy party" to describe the wonderful time our baby had playing with the substance he had suddenly discovered, to his immense interest and obvious delight, in his diaper. I had many letters from people who said they loved that euphemism, and no one needed to have it defined.

I think we should use more euphemisms, not fewer, especially now that writers insist on being so *explicit*. Now we all know the correct names of the various hitherto "private" (unfortunately, they haven't been private for years) parts of the human anatomy, so certainly euphemisms would not be misunderstood. In my opinion, unless one is writing a medical journal or a dirty novel, one shouldn't mention those "parts" at all.

A word that simply cries out for a euphemism, or even a metaphor would do, is POSSLQ, a Bureau of the Census connotation for Persons of Opposite Sex Sharing Living Quarters. Now I realize that half the parents in America were desperately seeking a nomenclature for their adult offspring's live-in lover (the half being mothers; fathers already had a word for it), but . . . POSSLQ? Surely there must be a better word! Some years ago a self-proclaimed bon vivant wrote to *Time* magazine suggesting that persons of the opposite sex living together are "co-vivants." (Don't knock the French; they gave us "derri-ere," which certainly sounds better than "bottom.") *Time* hailed "co-vivant," but it never caught on. A shame; it says it so well.

And for heaven's sake, let us find a better euphemism for "sexual activity" than "sleeping together." I recall the reply a widow friend of mine gave when asked if she was "sleeping with" her seventy-year-old gentleman friend.

"No," she said, "in fact, I'm not even sure he still sleeps!"

"Sleeps," to the ultraconservative, middle-aged square (another euphemism for me) has become a dirty word.

So, it would seem, has "adult."

When I was visiting in a small town recently, I wanted to buy a mystery novel to take home to my husband, but I became frustrated by the fact that every bookstore I went into sold only children's books. I finally asked a salesclerk, "Aren't there any adult bookstores in this town?" And she replied, "Not anymore; the sheriff closed it down!"

So I now need yet another euphemism for myself. You don't think I'm going to admit I'm an "adult," do you?

Part Three

It's All in the Game

20

WITH A FACE LIKE THAT, SHE NEEDS A MINK COAT!

My neighbor Nancy is recovering from a broken elbow she got during the Cabbage Patch craze. Nancy had already bought her daughter the Cabbage Patch doll, but when the local department store announced that they had Cabbage Patch accessories, Nancy, along with several thousand other women, dashed to the store to buy the latest CP accessory: a car seat. (Though at last count only four states required such restraints for the Cabbage Patch doll.) As Nancy picked up the car seat, another customer jumped her, grabbed the car seat, and screamed, "This one's mine! I touched it first!" In the struggle, Nancy's arm and elbow were smashed.

"I know it sounds awful," said Nancy the next day, "but actually I was pretty lucky."

"You mean because it was a clean break?" I asked.

"No," said Nancy, "as a matter of fact, the bone splintered. But in the confusion the woman ahead of me fainted and I was able to grab not only her car seat, but also her place in line!"

"Nancy!" I cried, "don't tell me you stayed there and stood in line with a broken elbow!"

"I had to," said Nancy. "They only had five thousand car seats left; if I had taken time out to so much as blink, they would have been sold out! If you had a daughter with a Cabbage Patch doll, you would have done the same thing, I'll bet!"

"You'd lose that bet!" I exclaimed, though even as I spoke that lie I recalled the Christmas I had trudged through a blizzard to buy a G.I. Joe doll complete with uniform, guns, bazooka, and tank for my four-year-old son.

Don't ask me why I did it. That little boy needed a warmongering doll about as much as I needed another little boy; in fact, he didn't even want a G.I. Joe, or so I assumed three days after Christmas when I found Joe in the hamper (where else? Four-year-old boys put everything in the hamper . . . except dirty clothes). Joe was missing not only his clothes, but also his arms and his legs and his costly accessories.

Why had I bought it?

Because it was a fad. All parents fall for fads (even God, evidently, who, at the height of the baby boom, kept sending me more little boys), and with ten children I probably fell for more fads than most mothers.

When my kids were little, I stood in line for Barbie dolls complete with Ken, clothes, camper, tennis racket, and tote bag.

I endured crowds and confusion and angry curses to buy a Fisher-Price playhouse with furniture, cars, people, and even a dog.

I leaped police barriers to get Bobby Sherman's album and poster and autograph and the pen he signed with.

I spent sixty dollars on raffle tickets for a Chatty Cathy doll which I didn't win and it was just as well, as somebody had stolen her coveted clothes as well as her tapes.

And I mortgaged my car for a Foos Ball table that everybody insisted they wanted, but nobody played because the balls were defective and nobody cared enough to replace them.

I'd like to think that I bought all those things to make my children happy, but what kid could possibly be happy with this latest fad: the lumpy, stumpy, stringy-haired, cabbaged-faced Cabbage Patch doll? ("Any kid," said my grown-up daughter with a sigh. "Remember Raggedy Ann?")

Whatever, I am glad that none of my grandchildren are "into" the Cabbage Patch fad, because you know what the latest accessory is, don't you? A full-length, silk-lined, genuine mink coat. Ridiculously expensive, but with that face and figure, the poor dear probably needs a mink coat.

Or at least that's the line my husband has been using for years.

21

THE JUNQUE JUNKIE

My French houseguest, Michelle, recently commented on the fact that the American automobile industry must be in trouble because "eet seems in every block, somebody has a garage for sale."

I explained that the springtime spurt of GARAGE SALE signs does not mean that garages are up for grabs, but rather, as a result of seasonal housecleaning, people are trying to get rid of their junk.

Are garage sales indigenous to America? Somehow I cannot imagine the English or the French—or certainly not the Japanese—lining their driveways with broken furniture, burned-out appliances, chipped chinaware, and Monopoly games missing most of the money, in an effort to unload them on unsuspecting bargain-seekers.

While I disparage the idea of cluttering up the neighborhood with garage sales, I also admit that come Saturday morning, I am the first bag lady out, cruising the area in search of just such a sale.

But I have an excuse; I'm an addict. (And if you think

it isn't possible to become addicted to garage sales, attend three in a row and then try to stop, cold turkey. You can't do it.)

I got "into" garage sales several years ago when, after a particularly greedy tornado tore through our town, I had the rather formidable task of replacing our home and everything in it. Replacing the house and the furniture was a snap compared to replacing all those incidentals one accrues over the years and forevermore takes for granted: clocks, colanders, can openers, scissors, sewing needles, etc., not to mention the mysterious miscellany that occupy one's Thing Drawer. (Talk about insecurity; just try living with an empty Thing Drawer.)

Someone suggested garage sales as a source for that stuff, and thus I was introduced to the world of ANYTHING ON THIS TABLE: TWENTY-FIVE CENTS and COLOR T.V., TEN DOLLARS, AS IS and WALNUT TABLE, POSSIBLE ANTIQUE, MAKE OFFER.

Every Saturday for weeks I went to garage sales, seeking such necessary items as kitchen gadgets and garden tools, mirrors and magazine racks, flashlights and placemats, and while it meant hours and hours of sifting through junk (or, as they prefer to call it, junque) I was able to find everything we needed, and more.

That was the problem: the more. Even though my house was filled, I couldn't stop. I kept buying more and more junque. I bought back scratchers and bud vases and pin cushions and playing cards, and an old-fashioned free-standing kitchen cabinet which I didn't have room for but I needed the extra Thing Drawer. I accumulated enough junque to hold my own garage sale, but I couldn't. Garage sales are held on weekends, and my weekends were taken up going to garage sales.

If you are thinking of getting "into" garage sales, I must warn you: don't. Especially now that the garage sale has moved indoors and changed its name to just sale, or worse, estate sale.

The estate sale may be more fun than the garage sale, since you can not only browse and buy, but you can also get a glimpse of that house you have always wanted to see the inside of, but they are more expensive. You may still be able to find a garden hoe for under a buck, but you will also find a Henredon sofa for nine hundred dollars, which is certainly a bargain, but you can't buy it even if you have the nine hundred dollars because you already have a perfectly good sofa.

This may lead you to thoughts of how to get rid of the sofa you already have, and the next thing you know you will be sitting on a lawn chair in the middle of your driveway haggling over the price of the treasures you have taken from your Thing Drawer because, of course, you can't sell just a sofa, you must also offer junque, as that is part of the promise when you advertise a sale. Are you really ready for an empty Thing Drawer?

If you do have such a sale, and find you can't bear to part with the things in your Thing Drawer, or if you run out of junque and need "a fix," call me. I not only deal; I deliver.

22

DON'T TELL ME!

My car developed a funny noise the other day, so I stopped in a service station to have it checked out. The mechanic peered under the hood, poked around a minute, then asked, "Ma'am, when was the last time you had the oil changed?" He didn't have to say another word; I knew immediately that he was going to sock me with a big repair bill.

Over the years there have been several simple, one-sentence comments that, however brief, have told me more than I wanted to know. The first was probably that single sentence that puts even the most self-confident child into a state of panic:

"Your teacher called." (Everybody over the age of four knows that teachers never call with good news.)

Another child-chiller is "Guess what? Grandma is giving us her piano!" (Do you know what a piano can do to the social life of a sixth-grader?)

The most provocative comments, however, are those made to adults. These include:

"Oh oh; what have we here?" (From the dentist, as he peers into your mouth.)

"Hmmm; I just may order that Mercedes after all." (From the orthodontist, as he peers into your child's mouth.)

"This is an old model, isn't it?" (From the repairman who is trying to get up the courage to tell you that although the only thing broken is a ninety-cent switch, they don't make them anymore, so it's goodbye, washer.)

"Will the owner of a black Cutlass, license number 1-2939, please come to the lobby?" (If all I did was leave the lights on, why is that policeman standing there with a ticket book in his hand?)

"The Nominating Committee asked me to phone you . . ." (It should be called the Coercive Committee.)

"Due to extreme weather conditions, the schools will close at noon. (That used to affect just the stay-at-home mothers; now the whole city has to shut down.)

"I didn't like that ol' school, anyway." (Whether this comment comes from a kindergartner who doesn't want to go back, a grade- or high-schooler who has been told he *can't* come back, or a college applicant reading her mail, you are in for one very bad day.)

"I just love college; I don't care if I ever graduate!" (The only thing scarier than having a child hate school is having one love it.)

"I'll pay you back; I won't forget; I promise!" (The "promise" means he won't forget, not that he'll pay you back.)

"Was my bike insured?" (The key word here is "was," as in "was my cashmere sweater supposed to be dry-cleaned?")

"Guess how fast our car can go?" (I don't want to know, and I don't want to know how he knows.)

"I have turned on the seat belt signs and asked the flight attendants to please be seated." (This, when you are still thirty thousand feet in the air and ninety minutes from your destination. What does he know that we don't know?)

"I'd like to speak to a parent or guardian, please." (You can die a thousand deaths before you find out the local library wants its books back.)

But I think the most chilling comment is the one every parent hears at one time or another from an offspring:

"Can we talk for a minute?" (If it was good news, he would have said it already.)

23

I DREAD OLD AGE!

I have always dreaded old age.

I cannot imagine anything worse than being old, maybe infirm, perhaps alone; just the boredom would do me in. How awful it must be to have nothing to do all day long but look out the window, or stare at the walls, or worse, watch TV.

So, last week, when the mayor suggested we all celebrate Senior Citizen Week by cheering up a senior citizen, I determined to do just that. I would call on my new neighbor, an elderly retired gentleman who had been recently widowed and had moved in with his married daughter because, I presumed, he was too old to take care of himself.

I baked a batch of brownies, and without bothering to call (some old people cannot hear the phone), I went off down the street to brighten up this old guy's day.

When I rang the doorbell the "old guy" came to the door dressed in tennis shorts and a Ralph Lauren polo, and he looked about as ancient and decrepit as Donny Osmond.

"I'm sorry I can't invite you in," he said when I introduced myself, "but I'm due at the Racquet Club at two; I'm playing in the semifinals today."

"Oh, that's all right," I said. "I baked you some brownies—"

"Great!" he interrupted, and snatched the box of goodies. "Just what I need for bridge club tomorrow! Thanks so much!"

"—and just thought we'd visit awhile. But that's okay! I'll just trot across the street and call on Granny Grady." (Now Granny Grady is not really my grandmother; she is just an old lady who has lived in our neighborhood forever, and everybody calls her "Granny.")

"Don't bother," he said. "Gran's not home; I know, I just called to remind her of our date to go dancing tonight. She may be at the beauty shop; she mentioned at breakfast that she had an appointment for a tint job."

At *breakfast?* Good Lord, this old guy and Granny couldn't be . . . oh, certainly not! Not at their age, they *couldn't!* . . . Could they?

I wished him luck with his tennis game (though I was much more interested in his game with Granny), and bid him good day.

But I am not easily discouraged. I had set aside that afternoon to call on somebody old, and by golly, I was going to find somebody old to call on!

I called my mother's cousin (age eighty-three); she was in the hospital . . . working in the gift shop.

I called my aunt (age seventy-four); she was in China . . . leading a tour.

I called my husband's uncle (age seventy-nine); I forgot; he was on his honeymoon.

And then I remembered old Sister Margaret, a nun

who had taught me in grade school. She had been living for years in a retirement home for nuns, and while I had visited her on occasion, it had been several years since I had seen her. I wondered if the old dear was too senile to remember me.

The old dear wasn't there.

"Who did you want?" the receptionist had asked when I had inquired if it would be convenient for me to call on Sister Margaret.

"Sister Margaret," I had repeated, wondering if the old nun had finally gone to God.

"Sister Margaret . . . Sister Margaret . . ." mused the receptionist. "Oh! You mean Mercedes! She's not here this week; she's on tour."

"Mercedes?" I asked. "On tour?"

"Mercedes is Sister Margaret's stage name," said the receptionist. "When she became an actress she took the name Mercedes because she had always admired Mercedes McCambridge and because she thought Mercedes sounded more seductive than Margaret."

"Sister Margaret . . . uh, Mercedes . . . became an actress?" I asked, too stunned to wonder when Sister had learned the meaning of the word "seductive."

"Actually, she's more of a producer-director," said the receptionist. "A couple of years ago, she organized a senior citizen's drama club and eventually it evolved into a caravan theater; they go all over the state putting on plays. But she'll be back Thursday . . . no, I'm wrong. She will be back, but she leaves that evening for Washington, D.C. She's on the White House Commission on Aging, you know."

No, I didn't know and I can't imagine how she got on

such a commission, since she obviously knows nothing about aging!

And I don't want to know about it, either!

I still dread old age, now more than ever. I just don't think I'm up to it.

24

WHEN THE HONEYMOON IS OVER

According to the results of a magazine quiz my husband and I took recently, our marriage is a bust. We are "totally unsuited to each other, and should a marriage take place, it won't last six months."

They were half right. My husband and I are unsuited to each other, but we have been married three hundred and sixty months, due, I suspect, to the fact that we are totally unsuited to each other.

I can't imagine anyone more boring than a "suitable" spouse who thinks like you do, agrees with everything you say or do, shares your talents, tastes, and goals, and never, ever, ever says, "I must have been out of my mind to marry you!"

Whatever would you talk about? Oh, I don't mean talk-talk, like:

"Wasn't that a great movie?"

"Absolutely."

"Terrific acting."

"Sure was."

"And beautiful scenery."

"Uh huh."

I mean TALK-talk, like:

"Wasn't that a great movie?"

"Great? Are you kidding? I fell asleep four times!"

"But the acting was so good!"

"You call that acting? I've seen better acting on Saturday afternoon wrestling!"

"Well you must admit the scenery was beautiful!"

"Oh no you don't; I'm not playing that game. I don't care how beautiful their scenery is, we're not going to Ireland next summer!"

You may prefer the "Uh huhs," but I rather enjoy the exclamation points.

My beloved and I have not always argued. There was a time, before we were married, when we agreed on everything. We both loved partying, and dancing. We both loved Italian restaurants, with their checkered tablecloths, stubby candles, and spicy sauces. We both loved going to football games on crisp, autumn afternoons, and going to old movies at our neighborhood theater. Argue? What about? We didn't have any money, in-laws, or kids; what else is there to argue about? (I know. Sex. But believe it or not, we didn't have any of that, either, though we did agree that it offered great promise!)

We agreed on everything. We even agreed we should get married.

Six months after the wedding we were disagreeing on everything except the existence of God and the fact that green was probably a good color choice for grass. Any other topic could start a spat.

I would get mad if he would refuse to take me to a party, or a dance, or a football game, or even a movie. (He said, "I don't like to go places. Why do you think I got married?")

He would get mad if I would go on a shopping binge and spend too much money. (He suggested I get a job; I said, "I don't like to work. Why do you think *I* got married?")

We argued about money, sex, the number of kids we should have, how they should be raised, which set of in-laws we should spend our holidays with, and all the usual domestic hassles.

Yet we have managed to stay married for thirty years. Obviously, we made some compromises on such things as:

Money. He is a saver and I am a spender, yet we both do our own thing. He puts our extra money in a savings account, and I sneak it out again and spend it. (Bored with your marriage? Try recarpeting the downstairs without having your spouse notice.)

Sex. Sex was everything it promised to be and more, unfortunately. Alas, every time he looked at me, I got pregnant. (You want to spice up your sex life? Play Vatican Roulette!)

Kids. (How many?) He wanted a big family and I wanted a small family, so we compromised and had ten children. (That's what is known as a Catholic compromise.)

Kids. (How to raise.) We argued for years about how to raise our kids and then suddenly realized they *were* raised. (You can't trust kids; they'll grow up while your back is turned.) We wasted a lot of time arguing, because actually, or so the sociologists say, a child's personality is developed by the time he is three years old. (The Jesuits used to say, "Give me a child till he is three, and I will save his soul," but that claim has never been proven simply because, in the history of the Society of Jesus, there has never been a Jesuit who could tolerate a two-year-old for more than ten minutes. That's why they become Jesuits.)

Holidays and in-laws. We only argued about that for four years, because by the fifth Christmas (with four sons) it was our in-laws who were doing the arguing. ("You can have them for Christmas, Helen, since we had them for Thanksgiving." "No, no, Hannah, you take them this year; we had them last year. It's only fair!")

On partying, dancing, dining out, going to movies and football games. I finally persuaded him to go to parties by promising him I wouldn't make him dance. He eventually agreed to resume dining out occasionally, especially when he realized the alternative was dining in with ten kids. We both agreed that movies and football games are more comfortably watched at home on TV, though we do manage to ignite a brief spark if his football game coincides with my movie.

All married couples argue; if they don't, they are either tired, bored, or newlyweds. Newlyweds naturally assume that they will never, ever argue or even disagree, but of course they will. It is inevitable that the honeymoon must end. But that's when the fun begins!

25

IT'S ALL IN THE GAME

A marriage expert at a Midwestern university recently researched thousands of married couples and concluded that "the happiest marriages are those that follow traditional patterns in which the wife is submissive to the husband, where she plays the subordinate role, arguing only about those issues which threaten their whole value system."

The "independents, on the other hand, are characterized by their commitment to freedom more than to each other; they fight about all kinds of issues because the real issue is who has the power."

I haven't researched the subject (aside from the fact that I have spent thirty years as a "submissive" wife), but I can tell you who, in marriage, has the power, and that is the spouse who is submissive.

I admit that I was brought up to be a "submissive" wife, and dutifully vowed to "obey" at my wedding. But after I had been married several years, I realized that if I took that particular vow literally, I would have, over the years, poured "concrete all over the damn lawn so we won't have to keep mowing it," stuffed "all that junk mail in the postman's ear," and killed "the next kid who takes my hairbrush out of the bathroom!"

Obviously, even the most submissive wife must use common sense.

Actually, the ideal marriage is not one where the wife is submissive; it is one where the wife makes her husband think she is submissive when, in fact, she is calling the shots. And she doesn't do this by arguing; she does this by playing the game. (Marriage is not, as so many believe, a battlefield where wars are won or lost or maybe mediated; it is a playground where the game goes on and on.)

For example, if the wife wants to recarpet the downstairs and the husband says, "We are not going to recarpet this downstairs now or at any time in the future!" it does not mean that the husband has won an argument. And it certainly does not mean that the downstairs is not going to be recarpeted. It simply means that the wife must make the next move, which will probably consist of moving the furniture so that the dog spots, coffee stains, and cigarette burns that she has heretofore so skillfully hidden are now glaringly noticeable to the one person in the house who drinks coffee, smokes cigarettes, and insists on keeping that aging, incontinent dog.

Not long ago, a dinner guest of ours suggested that I must be the dominant spouse in our family and I assured him that was not so; my husband is head of the family and he has the final say-so in everything.

My husband almost choked on his chicken. "If I make all the decisions," he said, "how the hell did we get this godawful flowered wallpaper?"

I reminded him that I had brought home four samples, and he had chosen that pattern himself. What I did *not* remind him was the fact that the other three samples were *really* godawful; how else could I get him to choose those gorgeous flowers?

If modern spouses truly want to achieve power, they should forget arguing and learn the secret phrase, which is "Yes, dear."

Nobody can argue with "Yes, dear." It is the final, perfect, squelch. The other spouse can rant and rave and present powerfully persuasive reasons why his wishes should be carried out, but the spouse who says, "Yes, dear," invariably gets her way.

Of course the "Yes, dear" must be followed by some magnificent mental maneuvering, but that's what makes marriage exciting and challenging, as every good game should be.

Just last spring, my husband issued the edict that our son, then a high school senior, would go to State, and not the faraway college of his choice. I didn't agree, but I said simply, "Yes, dear," because I knew I had time to formulate my game plan.

Throughout the summer I mentioned all the problems at State. I remarked how our grocery bills would decrease when our son went to college, though alas, being so close, at State, he would probably come home for dinner. I reminded my husband that the faraway college was his own alma mater and it would have been nice to have an excuse to go back for football weekends. I didn't argue; I just made mild, positive statements in favor of our son's choice.

Then one morning, when I knew my husband was getting ready to leave for a very important, long-planned meeting, I said:

"Honey, I really think we should reconsider that college choice. He really wants to go to your alma mater, and frankly I want him to go there. But of course the decision is yours; you are the head of the family. What do you say? May he apply to your old college?"

And do you know what that conniving, sneaking spouse of mine said? He said, "Yes, dear."

Now I have to figure out if he really meant it, or if he was just playing the game!

26

THE SCRUNCHED-UP SOCKS

Dear Abby once ran a letter from a wife complaining that her husband has a habit of tossing his dirty socks into the laundry, all scrunched up and turned inside out. While the wife admitted that this is a petty problem, it is, she said, driving her wild.

Abby replied that it "certainly is petty," and that any wife who truly loves her husband would willingly set his socks aright before washing them.

As might have been expected, Abby was deluged with letters from sock-washers and sock-wearers of both genders taking sides in the matter.

As a devoted wife who hates handling dirty socks but does it anyway, I was delighted to learn that wives are finally speaking out against this disgusting trait, though I was not surprised that husbands are still refusing to cooperate. What I did find surprising was that nobody has tried to turn the topic into a psychological issue, which, of course, it is.

Why *do* husbands toss their dirty socks into the laundry all scrunched up and inside out? Is it just laziness, or does it have some deeper meaning? Is it a husband's way of expressing male dominance? Is he trying to tell his wife that, despite the women's movement, in *their* household she is still the handmaiden? (Not likely; if he was that chauvinistic he wouldn't toss his socks into the laundry at all; he would just leave them on the floor, or maybe even kick them under the bed.)

I'd hate to think that any husband would actually take pleasure in watching his wife wince as she shoves her delicate little fingers into his filthy, foot-long knee-high to turn it right side out for laundering. I'd prefer to think that he is just thoughtless. On the other hand, maybe he is testing her, hoping that she will show some spirit and say something. (Some spouses come home from a frustrating day at the office just *aching* for a good argument.)

Or perhaps it is simply a game with him, sort of like Russian roulette, seeing how many scrunched-up inside-out socks he can "shoot" before she explodes.

And what about the wife? Why *doesn't* she explode? Does she enjoy playing the martyr, or is she just a pushover? Why doesn't she rebel? Toss the socks back? Suggest that he wash them himself? (I have heard rumors of husbands who do wash their own socks, and one wild story about a husband who once washed his wife's panty hose, but there is no documentary proof of such phenomena.)

Surely there is more to this dirty sock issue than meets the eye (or, in the case of two-day socks, the nose). Perhaps there should be a survey made, asking such pertinent questions as:

"At what age do men establish this disgusting habit?" (Certainly not as children; children don't change their socks, if in fact, they even wear them.)

"Does marriage do something to male sock-wearers?" (Does he miss his mama?)

"Would his mother defend his thoughtlessness?" (Probably.)

"Is she responsible for it?" (Probably not.)

"Does she sympathize with her daughter-in-law's feelings in the matter?" (Of course!)

"Will she speak to her son about it?" (Of course not!)

I must admit that my husband is one of those men who tosses his socks into the laundry all scrunched up and turned inside out, but he claims there is no psychological reason for this. He says, "that's just the way they come off my feet."

Nor am I making a statement when, after dutifully washing his socks, I return them to his bureau, fresh and clean, but in the same shape he gave them to me: all scrunched up and turned inside out.

That's just the way they come out of the laundry.

27

THE BODY TALKS

I just read an article on Body Language (or Kinesics, as it is called by those who can pronounce it) and I wish I hadn't. I will never again be able to twitch my nose or tap my toes without worrying that someone will misinterpret my thoughts, or worse, interpret them all too correctly.

The problem with Body Language is it's so logical. A person who stands with her arms folded, clutching her own elbows, may well be feeling, as the book says, insecure. On the other hand, she may just be cold, but that, too, is something she is saying in Body Language ("Why doesn't the host turn up the heat?").

It isn't just the way you fold your arms or tap your feet that tells the world what you are thinking or how you feel, it is also the way you move your whole body, and in which direction. According to that article on Body Language, all my friends know something I didn't know, and that is: My marriage must be in deep trouble because my spouse and I "split up" at cocktail parties. When the husband heads in one direction and the wife in another, it is obvious that they are trying to avoid each other, and are, in fact, seeking companionship elsewhere. Often the wife settles with one group, where she stays throughout the entire party, while the husband roams about, looking for an attractive female to latch onto.

Isn't that incredible? That is so true! My spouse and I always split up at cocktail parties; as soon as we walk in the door he heads for the buffet and I head for the bar. (It used to be the other way around, but that's what liberation will do for you.) And I *do* settle with one group, though I never before knew I was "avoiding my husband"; I thought it was just because I had finally found a chair. And while I hate to admit it, he most certainly does roam about until he finds a female to latch onto, though I must say he doesn't care how attractive she is as long as she keeps her hors d'oeuvres tray full.

Body Language is really quite intriguing. Did you know that when your spouse comes home from the office he (or she) can tell what kind of a mood you are in just by watching the way you move your hands and feet? It's true! My husband came home the other evening to find me beating one of the kids and kicking one of the dogs and he knew right away that I was not in a good mood.

One can even ascertain the state of a couple's marriage by observing the way they are seated at the family dinner table. If the husband sits at the head of the table, he is "obviously head of the household." If the wife sits directly opposite him, "they are in direct conflict over the dominant position." If the wife sits on her husband's right, however, "the marriage is ideal." I don't know how they figure that (and God knows what it would mean if she sits on his left; something subversive, no doubt), but I think it's a great idea because they can then hear each other over the chattering of their children. (Do you have any idea how difficult it is to carry on a dinner table conversation with your spouse when you sit at opposite ends of the table and you're separated by ten children?)

Actually, I do sit at the opposite end of the table, but this is the first time I knew that I was "in direct conflict over the dominant position." (The feminists would undoubtedly say that my body language is simply stating my equality.) I always thought I sat there because it is the seat closest to the kitchen. (And we know what that says, in *any* language.)

There is one theory of Kinesics that just might save my allegedly troubled marriage. The article went on to say that "a homemaker who is meticulously neat, keeping a spotless home with a place for everything and everything in its place, is too tense and uptight to be any fun. An untidy, relaxed atmosphere makes for a much happier home."

I'm certainly glad to know that. I just hope that when my husband comes home and finds the breakfast dishes still in the sink, the laundry stacked in the upstairs hall, and the manuscript for my next book spread all over the dining room table, he will realize how happy he is.

28

"... AND NOTHING BUT THE TRUTH, SO ... HELP ME, GOD!"

I would make a terrible witness.

If I ever have to testify in a court of law, I have no doubt that I will either be held in contempt of court for repeatedly claiming that "I don't remember!" or jailed for perjury because I thought I remembered when I didn't.

I was involved in an automobile accident one time and when my husband asked me to describe the driver of the other car, I said, "Well, he was quite tall, had gray hair, and looked like he was about fifty years old."

When the accident report later indicated that the fellow was "five four, blond, and thirty-nine years old," my husband asked me how I could possibly be so wrong. I said:

"Listen, when you are five foot one, *everybody* is tall! And of course that fellow claimed to be blond and thirty-nine; what gray-haired fifty-year-old man doesn't?"

It's not that I don't observe people, places, and things, or that I am not interested in them. On the contrary, after spending two decades housebound with ten kids, I delight in meeting people, going places, and seeing things. My interest and my powers of observation are in fine fettle. It's my memory that's fading . . . indeed, if it was ever in focus.

I am the type of person who can go into a restaurant, chat with the waitress for a while before giving her my order, then, ten minutes later, can't remember what she looks like . . . or what I ordered. (Though it is to my credit, I claim, that I can almost always remember *if* I have ordered.)

I can come home from a wedding, where I commented on the beautiful bridesmaids' dresses, and not remember what style or even what color they were.

I can read a book, enjoy it immensely, and tell all my friends they absolutely must read it . . . though for the life of me I can't remember why.

I have been known to walk into an airport, note on the monitor that my flight is number sixty-seven leaving from gate forty-two, get on the escalator, go through security, walk down the corridor, and wonder why flight forty-two isn't even listed at gate sixty-seven.

I can watch a television gourmet give a step-by-step demonstration on how to prepare the simplest entree, and not remember one ingredient. (I love to watch Jeff Smith or Julia Child whip up those elegant meals, which is why my husband tells people that "As far as Teresa is concerned, cooking is a spectator sport.")

Since I have become a lecturer, which means traveling all over the country meeting people, my husband says I really must improve my memory for faces, names, and personalities.

"You should practice," he said. "When you meet somebody new, take special note of their name, their occupation, their clothes, their voices, what they have to say. Then try to find one particular quality that makes them memorable."

That night, when he came home from work, he asked me if I had practiced.

"I did indeed," I told him. "I didn't go out, but somebody came to the door. She was a little girl, about eight or nine years old, distinctively dressed, soft-spoken, yet also very persuasive. She attends a nearby grade school, and participates in extracurricular activities."

"That's wonderful!" said my husband. "How did you remember all that?"

Actually, I didn't. I barely remember somebody ringing the doorbell. But where else would I have gotten twelve boxes of Girl Scout cookies?

29

THOSE GOLDEN YEARS

Psychologists would have us believe that the stability of a marriage is determined within the first five years of marriage. If you can make it through the fifth wedding anniversary, you're set for life.

Not true. The stability of marriage, as any senior citizen can tell you, is not truly tested until after the fortieth year of marriage, when, all too often, the husband has retired from his job. Any couple can love each other mornings and evenings and all through the night. It's daytime togetherness that strains the bonds of wedded bliss.

I have one friend who was happily married for forty-two years. Then, six months after her husband retired from his legal practice, she sued him for divorce on the grounds of "incompatibility." On the other hand, I know another woman who, eight months after her husband took "early retirement" (at age seventy-five; he swears he could have gone another ten years, and I believe him), she sued for separation on the grounds of too much "compatibility."

("The old goat must be in his second youth," she complained. "I haven't been so 'handled' since our honeymoon!")

My own husband is still years from retirement (thanks be to God), so I have yet to experience the frustration of what to do with an out-of-work spouse, but I have the feeling that if he ever does retire, he will never complain about being bored. This does not mean that he won't *be* bored; it just means he won't dare admit it, because if he does, I have enough tasks lined up to keep him busy from here to eternity, literally. For starters (and maybe forever), he can balance my checkbook.

But I have older friends whose husbands have retired, and I asked them what their husbands do all day. Please note that while these answers are true to life, the names have been changed to protect not them, but *me*.

HELEN: What does Ed do all day long? He follows me around the house telling me what I am doing wrong. "That's not the way to unload a dishwasher!" "What a stupid way to make a bed!" It doesn't really bother me, though; he's sort of like little Eddie, when he was a toddler. If he's underfoot, I know he's not getting into things.

JUNE: We travel, and we are thoroughly enjoying ourselves. Do we argue over flight schedules, hotel accommodations and restaurant prices? Oh no, never. You see, we don't travel together. When he goes to Las Vegas, I go to Phoenix. When he goes to Canada, I go to Mexico. We just got back from a grand trip; he went to China and I went to Europe. Retirement is really working for us!

MARILYN: What retirement? Has Bill retired? Good Lord, I'd better rush home and see what he's up to!

BETH: Since Harry retired, he has taken an intense interest in volunteer work. He spends hours every day calling either the hospital, the Y, the community center, or the parish pantry to find out how much longer I am going to be there and when the hell is he going to get any dinner.

AGNES: I just treat Tom the way I treated the kids years ago. Every morning I hand him a lunch box and his golf clubs and tell him not to come home before three-thirty.

GRACE: I don't have any idea what George does all day. Ten days after he retired, I went to work. Oh, we can live on his pension all right; we just can't live on his pension in peace!

SYLVIA: Sam has always been interested in electronics, so he keeps busy trying to repair all the old radios we have accumulated over the years. Someday I may even tell him where I hid the transistors.

SARAH: You know Walt's retired, and I know Walt's retired, but I don't think anybody has told Walt that Walt's retired. Every morning he goes down to the plant, and every afternoon he comes home complaining that "nobody down there pays any attention to me anymore; I oughta fire the whole bunch!" Why don't I remind him that he's retired and should stay home for a change? Do you think I'm crazy?

NELL: It's true that Ted is retired now, but he has a full-time job at home. You know we have eleven children, forty-seven grandchildren, and nine great-grandchildren. Ted keeps track of my birthday book.

ANN: *(Blushing)* It's none of your business what we do all day!

121

CYNTHIA: Arthur? Arthur who?

I am really not worrying about my own husband's retirement years, but I firmly believe that he will never retire. In the unlikely event that he ever does conclude that he is not indispensable and maybe someone else can run that company, I know how I would like to spend those golden years. We will:

- Do nothing. For at least three days, I want to watch him do nothing.
- Take long walks in the morning when the world is fresh and lovely, not at night when he is exhausted from working all day.
- Take our grandchildren to the park, the zoo, the children's museum, anywhere, while they are still young enough to want to go places with Grandma and Grandpa.
- Travel (together!).
- Talk to each other, for as long as we want, without interruption, about everything except his recent job.
- Listen to music, to all those albums we have purchased over the years but never taken time to really enjoy.
- Maybe even watch the soaps on TV (and either get interested, or laugh like crazy).
- Read aloud to each other (and not just from the newspaper).
- Have dinner with our grown children, one couple at a time, or with our unmarried children, one at a time, so we can sit back and listen, just to them.

Who knows? I may even let him teach me how to load the dishwasher and make the beds.

But I was just kidding about the checkbook. If we're married a million years, I'm not going to let him see my checkbook.

Part Four

THREE CHEERS FOR THE MSS.!

30

THREE CHEERS FOR THE MSS.!

Because I have a tendency to take issue with people who espouse such radical causes as revising the Scriptures to bisexualize the Blessed Trinity, or revising the entire English language to eliminate such sexist terms as "chairman," "mankind," and, indeed, any person-type word incorporating the suffix or prefix "man" (will "women" one day be "wos"?), I am often accused of being antifeminist.

The accusation is false. It is true that I was once reluctant to accept "equality" (having been raised to believe women were superior, I resisted stepping down), but once I realized that the feminists would not insist that I get a job, while they *would* insist that my husband help with the housework, I jumped onto the bandwagon.

Actually, as far as the feminist movement is concerned, I suppose I stand about halfway between Betty Friedan and Phyllis Schlafly, which, when you think about it, is a good place to stand because you are far enough away from both of them that you can't hear either one of them.

While I admit to objecting to such feminist-inspired tongue twisters as "chairperson" and "humankind," I also acknowledge that they have improved on many aspects of our language, not the least being (or maybe it is the least, but I like it anyway) their creation of the title "Ms."

I can almost hear proud maidens and even prouder matrons gasp at the thought of being, however inadvertently, addressed as "Ms.," but the fact remains, it is a logical title in an era when women now receive as much business correspondence as men.

Any writer can tell you of the turmoil we used to endure while trying to ascertain the marital status of a female editor. If the "Patricia Kossmann" (to whom we have been directed to mail our manuscripts) is married, will she reject our work because we dared to assume she is single? On the other hand, if she is a career-dedicated woman who exults in single bliss, will she hate us forever for calling her "Mrs."?

"Ms." is a marvelous alternative, and I am grateful to the thoughtful feminist who suggested it. I might add, however, that as a wife and mother who has made a career of writing about her husband and children, I EXPECT TO BE ADDRESSED AS MRS.

Another feminist-inspired suggestion that seems to make a lot of sense is the hyphenated last name. My husband shudders at the thought that, had our children been born a decade or so later, they might have been tagged "Burrowes-Bloomingdale," but I rather like the idea of a wife retaining her maiden name by prefixing it to that of her husband. True, it will louse up computers everywhere, and will boggle the minds of twenty-first-century children who must sign their names "John Smith-Jones-Powers-Cooney-Burrowes-Bloomingdale-Ad-

Infinitum," but at the same time it will eliminate the necessity of asking (on hearing of, say, Mrs. John Smith), "Who was she?" As if, on marrying, she ceased to exist.

As the feminists have been so good to give women an alternative title, as well as a custom whereby we can retain our revered maiden names, perhaps they will go one step further and get us out of those parentheses!

Am I the only wife who resents being parenthetical?

For years I have been parenthesized. No fewer than eleven home and school rosters have identified me as "A. Lee Bloomingdale (Teresa)." The Nebraska Bar Association lists me as "Arthur L. Bloomingdale (Teresa)." In the parish directory I am "Lee Bloomingdale (Teresa)." Even my mother has been known to address our Christmas card "Mr. and Mrs. A. Lee Bloomingdale (Teresa)" to segregate, she says, from my mother-in-law, Mrs. Arthur Lee Bloomingdale, Sr., Hannah, and my daughter-in-law, Mrs. Arthur Lee Bloomingdale III (Karen). (No one, least of all I, would dare to parenthesize my mother-in-law.)

I have seen my name parenthesized so often I'm surprised people don't expect me to autograph my books "(Teresa) Bloomingdale."

My husband claims that I overreact to those parentheses; that, after all, it is a logical way of identifying me as his spouse. But if that is the case, why did he get so upset when my college alumnae newsletter identified him as "Teresa Burrowes Bloomingdale (Lee)"?

Would he have preferred "Mr. Teresa Bloomingdale"?

Or better yet, "Mr. Teresa Burrowes"?

Yes, there are times I could give the feminists a rousing cheer, but since I'm stuck in the middle, I doubt they would hear me.

31

IT'S ABOUT TIME!

How sweet it is! It was a long time coming, but at last we shall have our revenge. Take *that*, Cheryl, Candace, Chrissie, and Dawn! Heads up, Alma, Ethel, Emma, and Florence! Our time has come!

According to a study made recently at Rensselaer Polytechnic Institute, a woman's name can influence her employment prospects. If she has a "nonsexy" name, such as Alma, Edna, Ethel or Ada, she can expect to advance to executive status. If she was christened Cheryl, Cindy, Heather, or Debbie, however, she may be doomed forever to the typing pool.

It doesn't make any sense, of course, and while male executives who control promotions will be the first to admit that, they are also the first to reject a Jill or a Jennifer in favor of a Mildred or a Myrtle.

The theory behind such thinking seems to be that girls with "sexy-sounding" names are airheads, while those with old-fashioned names are brighter (due, no doubt, to the fact that the Jills spent their school years dating, while the Ethels stayed home and studied).

While I admit that the whole idea is absurd and unfair, I also admit to being secretly thrilled that Mitzy and Melanie are finally gonna get theirs!

When I was growing up, I was an Ethel. Actually, I wasn't an Ethel, I was a Teresa, but you know what I mean. I certainly wasn't a Mitzi, or even a Carol. Did I get elected class president? (Of course not; that went to Amy.) Or homecoming queen? (With two Beths and a Shari contending? Are you kidding?) Or even a cheerleader? (Aw, c'mon; even I can't imagine a cheerleader named Teresa.)

There were a lot of Ethels in my day, which may explain why so many of us sought individualism by adopting nicknames. Cissy, Libby, Happy, Billie, and Mimi knew they could never make it as Cecilia, Elizabeth, Helen, Wilhelmina, and Mary Lou.

We girls with the "sensible" names were not surprised when, once out of college, the girls with the "sexy" names got all the best jobs, even though they could neither type nor take shorthand nor even add a simple column of figures. (I hasten to add, however, that such inadequacies were not due to the fact that they were airheads, though, to be honest, a lot of them were. They had simply been too busy filling their date calendar and collecting fraternity pins to concentrate on a "who-wants-one-anyway" career.)

Since we "sensibles" spent most of our young lives watching the "sexies" have all the fun and still get the jobs, you would think that when we got married and had daughters of our own we would have given them such promising names as Cynthia, Andrea, or Drue, but we didn't. We followed that age-old tradition that daughters should be named for either a saint or an aunt (preferably both) and thus named our girls Mary, or Margaret, or Alice, or Ann, forcing the poor dears to seek their own individualism by signing themselves "Mari," or "Peg," or "Alyce," or even "A.C."

I think perhaps we were the last of the "sensibles," however, for less than a decade later parents were naming their daughters Chastity, Sunshine, Moon Unit, and Rain (who will probably grow up to sign herself "Rayne"). It will be interesting to see how these rock-star-bred names will compete with those chosen by soap opera fans and readers of romance novels: Brooke, Blythe, Tiffany, Tawny, and Tor.

Frankly, I am not surprised that male employers would hire a Clara over a Kim, a Florence instead of a Fawn, a Rosemary rather than Rye. What would you expect of a clique christened James, John, Arthur, Francis, William, or George?

I am tempted to apply for a job, just to see how a Teresa would be treated, but I'm no airhead; I'm going to wait until an Ethel becomes chairman of the board.

32

THE FEMALE ECONOMIST

Last night my husband and I attended a fund-raising banquet, one of those affairs where, for the price of a new winter coat you probably wouldn't have bought yourself anyway and certainly won't now, you are served Panic Prime Rib (so called because the dinner committee panics if the cocktails drag on) and given the opportunity to hear (assuming you are still awake after the welcoming address, committee reports, honorary awards, and inevitable slide presentation) a celebrity speaker.

The speaker last evening was an internationally renowned economist who, unfazed by the fact that it was now past my bedtime, rattled off ninety minutes' worth of financial facts and statistics, most of which were Greek to me.

There must have been a lot of Greeks there, however, for the speaker was frequently interrupted by enthusiastic applause, and at the conclusion, received a standing ovation. (Though I have always suspected that audiences stand to "ovate" so they can get out of there faster.)

"Wasn't he terrific?" commented my husband as we made our way to the parking garage.

"Are you kidding?" I asked. "I thought he was dreadful; all he did was rattle off a bunch of statistics."

"Of course," he said, "that's what made him so fascinating. Gads, what a mind that man has; he must know everything there is to know about the economy!"

I admitted that the man knows a great deal (certainly more than I cared to hear), but he obviously doesn't know *everything* about the economy, or he wouldn't have left out some of the most pertinent facts, a few of which I offer here:

On any given weekend, two out of every three teenagers in America will ask their father for money. (The other third will ask their mother.)

When investing in the stock market, it will make no difference if you "buy high" or "buy low"; once that stock realizes it is *yours*, it will sink into oblivion.

Conversely, if you sell a stock, you can count on the fact that it will rise three points the moment it leaves your portfolio.

Before investing any money in the stock market, ask yourself one question: How many rich stock brokers do you know? (Buy bonds.)

While it is true that the interest on tax-free bonds need not be reported to the IRS, it is still a good idea to keep a record of the coupons clipped and deposited, for your accountant or spouse (which are all too often the same person) is going to expect you to remember what you did with that thirty-four-dollar-and-nineteen-cent windfall you got twice last year. (The fact that it was swallowed up in your checking account is not an acceptable answer.)

Given a five-dollar bill and sent to the store for a three-fifty purchase, eight out of ten children will account for the change as follows: (a) "I lost it," (b) "The man didn't give me any change," (c) "I thought you said I could buy some candy and soda." Two out of ten will never get to the store, and on returning home will ask, "What five dollars?"

When a man and a woman of equal talents and abilities both apply for the same job, in ninety-nine cases out of one hundred the one hired will be the one who is related to the chairman of the board.

While the cost of raising and educating a child is now estimated at approximately one hundred thousand dollars, it is to be noted that this does not include the following: bubble gum, bicycle repairs, gasoline, the senior prom, or "incidental expenses" incurred as an active member of a college fraternity or sorority. (On the other hand, maybe that's what it *does* include, and everything else is "incidental.")

When investing in money market funds, certificates of deposit, Treasury bills, or savings accounts, remember that old adage "A penny saved is a penny taxed."

Which leads me to conclude with the wisest financial advice anyone has ever offered:

If you've got it, spend it.

33

BLOOMINGDALE, THE BON VIVANT

A New York University professor recently assigned his English students an essay on how each would spend a day as a member of the opposite sex. Our metropolitan daily picked up this story, and conducted a contest, challenging readers to submit their own essays on the subject.

As a writer, I felt compelled to participate, but as a woman who has, in the past two decades, lived with no fewer than eight men (one husband and seven sons—good heavens, what did you think?) I found it difficult to choose the age I would want to be, if I could be a man for a day. Would I want to be a teenager? A young man in my midtwenties? A middle-aged executive?

Since I cannot remember my teens, and will not admit to middle age, I chose the midtwenties; I would be a Yuppie ("young urban professional"), unmarried, successful, wealthy, a bon vivant.

Were I a young bachelor living alone (surely some bachelors still live alone!), I would wake each morning to the ring of the telephone, the light-of-my-life calling to say, "Good morning, handsome! I just wanted to remind you of our date for lunch." (Quite an improvement over what used to be reveille: "Get up, jerko; you've already missed breakfast!")

After a lengthy shower, with nobody complaining that I'm using all the hot water, I would don a Hickey-Freeman suit (enhanced with Hathaway shirt and Countess Mara tie), breakfast on black coffee and croissants, and then call my doorman to send round my Mercedes. Or perhaps, if the weather is pleasant, I would walk downtown to my office on Wall Street. (Of course I live in Manhattan; where else would a Nebraska mother imagine her sex-switched self to be?)

I would spend a busy morning advising Averill, Walter, Bunny, and other fellow bankers, dash off a note to *The Economist* thanking them for the interview (though I wish they hadn't called me a "boy genius"; after all, I am hardly a boy), and chat with David Rockefeller on the phone.

At noon I would saunter into the Four Seasons, wave to Walter Cronkite, say hello to Henry Kissinger, and hope the Sinatras don't see me because after all, I can't stop to talk to just anybody. I would find my date already seated at my regular table, and we would lunch on quail or lobster, with just the right wine (I am a connoisseur of fine wines), and though she might consider it chauvinistic, I would insist on picking up the tab, paying with my exclusive Gold Card.

After walking her back to her prestigious law firm (she's a full partner there; as my father used to say, "If you can't date Inherited Wealth, Successful Career is a suitable substitute"), I would decide that the autumn afternoon (it's always autumn in a Nebraskan's fantasy) is too glorious to spend in an office. So I would call another light-of-my-life, suggest we go sailing, then report to my office that for the rest of the afternoon I could be reached through my yacht club.

At dusk we would return to the city, where I would put my friend in a cab and go home to shower and change for my evening's engagement with still another "light." (Why do you think I moved to Manhattan?)

I would meet her for cocktails at Elaine's, take her to dinner at 21, then let her decide: Should we attend the Celebrity Gala at Lincoln Center (it's "By Invitation Only," but of course I have one) or should we catch Bacall's new play at the Palace? (SRO? No problem; Betty always saves seats for me.)

After the play and a nightcap at Sardi's, I would leave my date at her porte cochere (yes, I mean *leave;* who do you think is writing this fantasy . . . Sidney Sheldon?) and return home to conclude the evening as every good son should, by calling my parents to inquire about their day, to give them my love, to bid them goodnight, and to request a small loan because the payments are due on my condo, my car, my clothes, and my Gold Card.

Alas, doesn't every fine fantasy end in reality?

34

MS. VICE PRESIDENT
(OR BETTER YET, MRS.)

Many people believe that the time has come to elect a woman Vice President of the United States, and despite the fact that I was once tagged "antifeminist" (because, when my tenth child started school and a feminist friend suggested that I could "now go to work," I threatened to kill her), I agree with them.

I have always thought that a woman would be ideally suited to be Vice President of the United States, especially if she has had previous experience as either (a) a daughter, (b) a wife, (c) a mother, or (d) a teacher.

Who could better fullfill the constitutionally stipulated role of "serving at the discretion of the president" than someone who has been serving at the discretion of somebody else since the day she was born? Certainly, the President would get a lot more cooperation from a woman Vice President, and without a doubt the Senate would be in far better shape if the gavel were held by a woman.

If a woman was presiding over the United States Senate, you can be sure that the senators would be *there*.

Senators are notorious for being absent from the floor; as any tourist can tell you, there are seldom more than six present at any one time, the exceptions being a declaration of war, a vote to increase salaries, and the anticipation of television coverage. No woman would tolerate such absenteeism. From the very first session she would insist that anybody absent three times in a row would not be allowed back on the floor without a written excuse from his spouse.

A woman presiding over the Senate would certainly curtail such senatorial bad habits as procrastination ("Get with it, guys, or nobody goes home!"), bickering ("Are you senators or sophomores?"), double-talk ("You speak with eloquence, Senator, but unfortunately, you don't make any sense."), and above all, spending ("Two million dollars to plan the five-hundredth anniversary of Columbus Day? Don't be ridiculous. The Sons of Italy will do it for nothing!").

As the Vice President also sits in on meetings of the President's cabinet, we would also save a bundle of money there ("Would the Attorney General like to tell us just what he expects to learn on this planned junket to Wimbledon?") as well as in the Security Council. ("Why do we need spies when we already have exchange students? My neighbor's daughter picked up more dirt in one semester than Blackford Oakes accumulated in four books!")

It goes without saying that a woman Vice President would be much better than a man in representing our government at such functions as state funerals, royal weddings, dedications, coronations, or for that matter, any event at all that involves more than six people or lasts past 9 P.M.

Yes, America would be wise to elect a woman Vice

President, assuming that she is a woman who *thinks* like a woman, and not like a man. But this is unlikely to happen, because a woman who thinks like a woman would have better sense than to let herself get talked into a job like that.

35

DO YOU KNOW . . . ?

I am bleary-eyed this morning because I stayed up late last night watching the Academy Awards ceremony on TV. I really didn't care who won; I had not seen any of the nominated movies, and I was familiar with only three of the stars anticipating Oscars. So why did I watch?

Because I had to attend a committee meeting this morning, and I was not about to walk into a roomful of my peers and not know who had won the Academy Awards. It would be tantamount to admitting, the day after a national election, that I didn't know who had won the presidency.

Over the years I have learned that if one is to be "accepted in polite society" (a phrase which has often made me wonder who did the "accepting," and wouldn't I rather try for "impolite society"), one simply must be knowledgeable of certain facts. These include, other than the Academy Award winners:

1. Who won the World Series. Now it makes no difference that you are not a baseball fan, never watch a

game, didn't follow the play-offs, and wouldn't know a Chicago Cub from a Chicago Bear. If you are over the age of six, you will be expected to know, in any given October, what teams are playing in the World Series, who made spectacular home runs, who threw temper tantrums, and who won. Not to know this minimal amount of information will class you immediately as a nerd.

2. The same goes for the Super Bowl. If you plan to attend any party, meeting, convention, or church during the month of January, be prepared to talk intelligently about the upcoming, or just played, Super Bowl. (On second thought, it is only necessary that you be prepared to talk, period. When discussing the Super Bowl, *intelligence* is not a requisite.)

3. What's going on on "Dallas" and "Dynasty." I assume there is no longer anybody out there who doesn't recognize the names J.R. or Alexis (though I held out for years, until I realized I wasn't being invited *anyplace*), but do you know who recently got blackmailed by a Ewing or blackballed by a Carrington? You don't? Well, don't panic; any seven-year-old can bring you up to date.

4. Today's target in "Doonesbury." It is now all right to admit that you read "Doonesbury" (though it is not yet acceptable to confess that you get a kick out of it), but to be truly "in the know" you must be aware of the current episode's "pickee." If one is not prepared to comment on what happened in "Doonesbury" today, one might as well be in a monastery. (Though I heard a rumor that one jolly monk periodically posts the strip on the refectory door.)

5. The ending of Sidney Sheldon's latest book. Can you imagine how embarrassing it is to be the only person

in the beauty salon who cannot nod knowingly when some-one says, "What did you think of Sidney Sheldon's latest book? Wasn't that ending a zonker?"

6. The latest love interest on "General Hospital." This is not to say that you must watch "General Hospital"; you just must know who is having an affair with whom. To obtain this information without subjecting yourself to two and a half hours a week of "soap," read the "soap opera" update in your weekend newspaper, or ask any college student. Remember the days when soap operas were watched surreptitiously? Now, it seems, soap fans have come out of the closet. I was lunching at the Officers' Club at SAC headquarters not long ago when I noticed a group of "stars"—majors, colonels, and generals—suddenly gath-ered around the TV set over the bar. I asked a waiter if there was a news bulletin on and he replied with a sigh, "No, madame; just 'All My Children.' " Let us hope the Russians don't decide to attack at noon.

7. At least 5,975 answers in Trivial Pursuit. Don't worry about this, however. If you know all of the above—movies, sports, cartoons, soaps, and sexy books—you will *know* all the answers in Trivial Pursuit.

And if you don't play Trivial Pursuit, you might as well be dead.

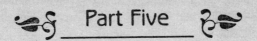

Part Five

POTPOURRI

36

Z-Y SOMETHING

I am terrified that any day now I will be arrested for drunken driving. The fact that I don't drink is irrelevant; I drive, and that's what counts. (Actually, I do drink an occasional glass of wine with dinner, but I never drive afterward. My kids claim that I don't even like wine; I just drink it so I'll have an excuse not to drive them anyplace after dinner.)

Whenever I drive, or for that matter, whenever I don't drive, I am as sober as a judge, which is a ridiculous comparison considering some of the judges I know, but for heaven's sake don't quote me because I will undoubtedly be coming up before one of them any day now.

Nonetheless, I am not a very good driver. I tend to switch lanes without signaling first, due to the fact that when I learned to drive, there was no second lane to switch to, and consequently no signal for such. I also cut wide corners because I can never remember to turn until I am halfway through the intersection, and I daydream at stoplights, causing much consternation when the light turns green and I don't go.

Since I am such an absentminded driver, any policeman would certainly be justified in pulling me over for a warning or even a ticket. But I have always been quite confident that none of them would ever question my sobriety.

Until now. No, I have not taken to excessive drinking; they have taken to unfair testing. According to a recent news report, henceforth any driver stopped for any reason at all will have to prove his or her sobriety by reciting the alphabet . . . backward.

Can you believe it? *Backward!* I don't know about you, but if I were in the middle of a busy thoroughfare, being interrogated by an armed officer of the law and gawked at by passersby, I'm not even sure I could recite the ABC's forward. I know darned well I couldn't recite them backward.

Since reading that report, I have been afraid to get behind the wheel of my car lest I make a mistake and end up in the jug.

It's not that I don't understand or appreciate what the police are trying to do. No one is more concerned than I about the number of automobile accidents caused by drunk drivers. I was a member of MADD (Mothers Against Drunk Drivers) when it was still called MAD (Mothers Against Drivers . . . especially those driving my car). I will cheerfully give the police my full cooperation, my taxes, my teenage sons! But not myself! I don't wanna go to jail!

A policeman friend of mine told me I am unduly worried.

"I know you are an erratic driver," he said, "but it is unlikely that you will ever be stopped, let alone arrested."

"Why do you say that?" I asked.

"You're too old!" he said, simply and truthfully. "We're

not out to get middle-aged matrons who are weaving their way to the grocery store at twenty-five miles per hour. We're after the young speed freaks. And then there's the time element. Most of our arrests are made after midnight on Friday and Saturday nights. Let's face it, Teresa; how often do you drive down Drag Strip, playing tag with your peers?"

"So it's the teenagers you're out to get!" I said.

"We're out to get any drunk drivers, or any drivers who are breaking the law. If kids are driving wildly, we're going to stop them, and if they've been drinking, we're going to arrest them."

"You may stop them," I said, "but you'll never arrest them."

"Why do you say that?" he asked.

"Because drunk or not, they'll pass the test!" I said. "Haven't you heard of the new teenage brain game? Every kid in high school has to learn the alphabet . . . backward!"

"So I'll make 'em recite it frontward!" he said huffily. "But we're gonna get those kids! If we see kids driving wildly, or being rowdy, or just making too much noise, we're going to do something about it. Maybe we can't arrest them, but we will call their parents and make them come and get them!"

Oh, swell. You know what that means, don't you? Until these kids of mine are grown up and gone, I'm either going to have to give up that glass of wine, or learn my Z-Y-X's!

37

WALKING CAN BE HAZARDOUS TO YOUR HEALTH

One evening last spring, my daughter the runner gave me a pat on my broadening behind and remarked that middle age was not just catching up with me, it was settling in on my back porch.

"You're getting a little hefty there, old girl," she said. "You need more exercise."

"I get plenty of exercise," I told her. "I've been up and down the basement steps a dozen times today."

"Oh, give me a break, that's not exercise," said she who hasn't been down in the basement in years. "I mean real exercise, like jogging, or running. Just look what running has done for me!"

I looked, and she definitely had a point. In the past year, my once chubby, adolescent daughter had run herself into lithe and lovely young womanhood. She hadn't even had to diet; by just running five miles a day she had slimmed down to the point where she was not only gorgeous, she glowed good health.

"You're right," I said. "But I can't run; I'm too old! I'd drop dead at the first intersection."

"Then walk!" she said. "Walking is just as good as running. You used to walk a lot, before Dad bought you that car. Now the only place you walk is to the garage and back. No wonder you're getting fat! Tomorrow is going to be a beautiful day; why don't you walk a mile before breakfast?"

I agreed to give it a try, and that I did. I tried. I hadn't gone three blocks before I remembered why I had given up walking in the first place: the hills. I swear, I live in the only city in the world where you can walk around the block and go uphill all the way. (And if you don't believe me, come to Omaha and walk around the block. Any block.)

There is a popular misconception in this country that Omaha, Nebraska, is flat prairie land. Wrong. Omaha, Nebraska, is as hilly as San Francisco; the only difference is, when you get to the top of a hill in Omaha you can't see the ocean.

In San Francisco, at least, a hill is easily recognizable as a hill; in Omaha you can be easily deceived. For example, there is a stretch of streets in southwestern Omaha that I have driven twice a day for years. If asked, I would have sworn that stretch was perfectly flat.

The first time I walked it I had to stop six times to catch my breath.

Despite the hills, I have become a walker (or if you will, a climber) and I love it. I love the quiet hour all by myself; I love breathing the fresh morning air; I love the "lift" which can only be understood by another walker; I love feeling that I am better than all those lazy loafers who are driving to their destination!

Yet I have also learned that there are cons to walking, some of them real hazards, such as:

1. All your neighbors will turn against you because (a) when they stop to offer you a ride you will turn them down, and they'll think you're a snob, and (b) they'll be right.

2. Unless your spouse is also into exercise, he, too, will begin to hate you because you look so great, and worse, you feel so young.

3. All those neighborhood dogs who have been cheerfully chasing your car for years and years will not recognize you on foot, and try to attack you for infringing on their territory. Dogs feel threatened by joggers, runners, and walkers, and why wouldn't they? The sidewalks have been theirs for aeons.

4. Walking is addictive; you will want to walk when you should be cooking, cleaning, fighting with your kids. You'll want to walk in the morning, after lunch, in the evening, late at night. If taken in great doses, walking can ruin your life!

So I gave up walking, not because it was hazardous to *my* health, but to my daughter's.

As the months went by, and I grew slimmer and slimmer, I noticed that my daughter was putting on weight.

I finally asked her what was causing it, and she said I was!

"It's your fault I'm getting fat, Mother!" she wailed. "Since you've been walking so much, your dear darling car has been just sitting and sitting in the garage, forgotten and neglected and ignored. Well, I couldn't let that happen, could I? I started driving it just around the block; then I took it to work; lately I drive everyplace! I haven't used my legs in weeks, and it's all your fault!"

So I am back to the lazy life of a suburban driver. It's the least I can do for my daughter.

38

THE GREAT INTIMIDATORS

Nobody intimidates me more than a high-priced hairstylist.

Wouldn't you think that a woman who has, over the years, been subjected to the rigid rules of an old-fashioned father, the sarcasm and sophistry of a lawyer-husband, the caustic complaints of smart-alecky teenagers, and the rejections and revisions of various editors would, by now, be immune to intimidation?

Actually, I thought I was. I considered myself a self-confident and sophisticated woman until the day I found myself in La Salon de Pierre, getting my hair "done."

I had been in beauty shops before, of course, but not for some years. When the price of a shampoo-set soared to the ridiculous price of four dollars, I decided I could "do" my own hair.

However, when my career as a writer and author expanded to include personal appearances on the lecture circuit and network TV, my spouse suggested that perhaps I should have my hair styled professionally, and maybe even colored as well. I agreed, so I called Bea's Beauty

Parlor, only to discover that Bea had sold out and the place was now called La Salon de Pierre.

That should have warned me. Nothing in French is cheap.

My suspicions were confirmed when I walked into the salon and saw a calligraphed sign stating: MANICURES BY MONIQUE: ONLY TWENTY-FIVE DOLLARS. (Only?)

If they charge twenty-five dollars just to polish my nails, what would they charge to color my hair?

I didn't dare ask. Somehow one knows, in a place like that, that one simply doesn't ask. To ask is gauche. If you cahn't afford it, dahling, you shouldn't be here.

What should I do? Walk out? God forbid. The only thing worse than asking is walking out.

I gave the receptionist my name, and was told to please be seated, M. Pierre would be with me in a moment. Forty "moments" later (this guy must think he's a doctor), M. Pierre sent his assistant to usher me to his alcove.

As I introduced myself, the coiffeur simply looked at me, closed his eyes, and sighed. What's the matter with him? Doesn't he enjoy a challenge?

He bid me be seated, and as he brushed through my hair, he said:

"May I ask what Madame uses for shampoo?"

You may ask, I thought to myself, but I'm certainly not going to tell you that I use bath soap because the kids have confiscated all the shampoo.

"I'm bored with my old shampoo," I said in my best bored-with-my-old-shampoo voice. "Why don't you try something new?"

"Certainly," he said, with obvious relief. "And the rinse? Madame's hair seems to have a unique aroma . . ."

Unique? What's so unique about vinegar?

"Whatever you think is best," I said. "I place myself in your hands."

The next thing I knew my hair was being shampooed, styled, cut, colored, and curled, and as the Great Coiffeur wielded his scissors and comb, I began to panic. Would I like the new me? More important, would I be able to pay for the new me?

After M. Pierre had put on the final touches, fluffing and spraying and admiring his artistry, he turned to me and said, "Now in the future, Madame, you must always use this particular shampoo and this particular rinse, both of which, fortunately for you, are available for purchase right here in this salon."

Of course I bought them, because I knew if I didn't every hair on my head would fall out. By the time I had tipped everybody who had touched my hair, my cash was depleted and I had to pay with a credit card. (God is good; I had not overcharged my limit.)

When I got home my husband said:

"Wow! You look gorgeous!"

"I should," I said. "It cost me enough."

"Expensive, huh?" he asked.

"Well," I said, "let me put it this way. From the scalp up, I am worth more than all the rest of me put together."

"Whatever, it was worth it," he said. "You look terrific! Now you should go out and buy yourself a chic new outfit to go with your chic new hairdo."

"No thank you," I said, because if there is anybody who intimidates me more than a high-priced coiffeur, it's a high-priced couturier.

Somehow I wasn't up to more intimidation.

39

LEFT VS. RIGHT

It seems that almost everyone has a Cause these days, protesting discrimination for one reason or another, and I am surprised that we haven't heard from one minority group who truly has a gripe: people who are born left-handed.

Now it is true that a few thoughtful lefties are manufacturing products for southpaws, but for the most part, it is still a right-handed world.

Take toys, for example. The pushbutton, the windup key, the horn on the tricycle, they are always on the hard-to-reach right. No wonder left-handed people become more aggressive; they learn frustration early in life.

In school it gets worse. Have you ever been in a classroom full of student chairs? Ninety-nine of them have the wide writing arm on the right; the two for left-handers are stuck back in the corner. (Why only two? And why there?)

If a left-handed boy wants to go out for sports, he will have to bring his own baseball glove because all the school mitts are made for right-handers. And God help him if he wants to play golf; left-handed clubs are available, but they are expensive and scarce, as are left-handed archery bows and left-footed bowling shoes.

As for bowling, he must, of course, have his ball specially drilled, because the alley balls are all made for his right-handed friends.

If a left-handed girl wants to become a seamstress, she must search long and hard for left-handed scissors. She'd be smarter to switch from left-handed to right, because there are no southpaw sewing machines made.

Guitars, violins, and pianos are also made for right-handers, as are typewriters, calculators, computers, and (unless you are British) automobiles.

Left-handed homemakers complain about can openers, potato peelers, and pot strainers that are awkward to use, as well as microwave ovens and refrigerators whose doors open in the wrong direction. (In fact, all doors are on the wrong side for the left-handed person.)

My left-handed sister, who is a teacher as well as a mother, complains that all teacher desks have right-handed drawers. She also finds it difficult, she says, to shake hands, dial a rotary telephone, cook with a portable mixer, iron anything at all (the cords are always in the way), or even to vote.

"To vote?" I inquired. "Why is it difficult for you to vote? We don't have voting machines."

"No," she said, "but we do have short strings. The pencil will never reach."

It's not just *things* that discriminate against the left-hander, it's also definitions and ideas.

The French word for "left," that is, *gauche*, has come to mean, in American, "awkward, tactless, clumsy, and lacking in social grace." (Or so says my right-handed dictionary. Books also discriminate; like doors, they all open the wrong way.)

The goody-goody right-handers, however, can claim to be *adroit* (from French *droit*, "right") or "skillful, deft, sharp, smart, and quick."

A left-handed compliment is one that is insincere; a left-handed Irishman one who does not go to church; a left-handed marriage is one that is considered unsuitable (e.g., the Duke of Windsor's).

But we all know what it means when the boss introduces his "right-hand man." (It means his left-hand man is back at his desk trying to work his right-hand computer.)

How do you think all this makes a left-handed person feel?

I wouldn't know, because I am right-handed, or, as the dictionary defines it: "on the right side, helpful, reliable, upright, correct, conservative, and clever."

Not bad for one who has never been able to tell her *gauche* from her *droit*.

40

I DIDN'T NEED TO KNOW THAT

When Princess Caroline of Monaco gave birth to her first child, the news media reported the exact number of months, weeks, and days since her marriage, making special note of the fact that they were considerably less than nine months.

I didn't need to know that. I didn't even want to know it. As a longtime fan of the late Grace Kelly, I would have liked to rejoice in the birth of her first grandchild without being made privy to the fact that while the pregnancy was premature, the baby wasn't.

There are, in fact, a lot of things I don't need to know, or want to know, and some I would definitely rather not know, such as:

1. Rose Kennedy's "idiosyncrasies" as "revealed" by her chauffeur.

2. John DeLorean's thoughts on religion.

3. The ending of *Star Trek IV*.

4. The ingredients of hot dogs, sausage, or bubble gum.

5. The latest celebrity to enter the Betty Ford Clinic for Drug Dependency.

6. If Princess Di and Prince Charles are really in love.

7. The metric system.

8. Whether or not Dolly Parton has had plastic surgery (though I would love to know what she looks like without a wig).

9. Who Burt Reynolds is currently bedding.

10. How much my husband paid for the bracelet he bought me for Christmas.

11. Six easy steps to wallpapering a dining room.

12. Why Katharine Hepburn never married.

13. How to make homemade spaghetti sauce. (Follow the directions on the jar.)

14. Frank Sinatra's age. (Whatever, it's "a very good year.")

15. Anything more about Marilyn Monroe.

On the other hand, there are zillions of things I would really like to know, such as:

1. How to lose twenty pounds without giving up chocolates.

2. Why television caters to the young when the young are all out sitting in bars (and their parents are at home being subjected to video rock).

3. If a twenty-five-year-old is still living at home, shouldn't he still have to obey his mother?

4. How to cook dinner for twelve in twenty-five minutes or less.

5. If I am going to enjoy a novel I am considering paying seventeen dollars for.

6. How to remove DO NOT REMOVE tags from sofa cushions without ripping open the cushions.

7. If my neighbor is going to share those luscious homegrown tomatoes or should I give up and go out and buy some.

8. How to get the brush cartridge off my vacuum cleaner (and how to get it back on again).

9. Why batteries come in packs of two or four when appliances call for one or three (and where did I put that extra battery?).

10. How a reasonably bright twenty-year-old college student could move out of a recently condemned campus apartment and not ask for his rent deposit back.

11. If it's too late to start lying about my age.

12. If it's worthwhile buying new tires for our seven-year-old station wagon, or is that coughing in the carburetor a death rattle.

13. Where I can buy size 5 1/2 AA shoes.

14. How to break the news to my husband of the impending death of our family refrigerator.

15. How to say no to my grandchildren.

While I did take exception to the detailed report of the royal birth in Monaco, I wouldn't want you to think that I am above enjoying a bit of gossip. Especially literary gossip. How can Father Andrew Greeley, who is a very holy priest and writes beautiful spiritual essays, bring himself to write those sexy novels? What does his mother think about that? What does *the Pope* think about that? Why, those novels are outrageous! They're filled with sex, and sin, and scandal!

(And does anybody know when the next one's due out?)

41

UNSUNG HEROES

As a sleek, late-model convertible zipped past us on the highway, my husband, who had been moaning about the amount of work that must have piled up during his absence from the office, said:

"Well, at least I don't have to do that!"

"Do what?" I asked. "Drive a convertible?"

"No," he said. "Design one. Or any other car. Do you have any idea what pressure auto designers must be under all the time? No sooner does one model come off the drawing board than the designers are expected to come up with another. How many times can one redesign the same make automobile? Yet year after year after year the designers are expected to come up with something new and exciting. The poor devils never get finished!"

I wondered how a father who had just deposited his eighth child in college and still had two to go could assume that *any* job ever got finished, but I knew what he meant. Automobile designers must have one of the most pressing and thankless jobs in the world, because for every person who says, "Gee, what a beautiful car!" there are nine critics who complain that the car is either too short or too long, too elaborate or too plain, or has too many gimmicks (a complaint which usually means "Gads, I'd love to have a car like that, but my wife would kill me if I spent that kind of money!").

Along with automobile designers, there are many unsung heroes in this world, none of whom I would want to be, but all of whom I admire greatly. For example:

1. The fellow who stands in the middle of a busy highway, redirecting traffic during road construction. Not only must he endure extreme weather conditions, but he must also subject himself to the possibility of being smashed to a pulp by a speed freak who doesn't know STOP from GO.

2. The dietician who must make up the school lunch menus. (If ever there was a "can't win" job, that's it.)

3. The ticket seller who must announce to a thousand fans who have been waiting in line since Tuesday that the Madonna concert has just sold out.

4. The department store clerk who must man the exchange desk the day after Christmas.

5. The tailor who fits my husband's suits. (All middle-aged men should have two wardrobes; one size for before meals, and one for after.)

6. The kindergarten teacher, on the first day of school. (Though the weeping and wet pants on this day are compensated for by the hugs and kisses on the last day.)

7. The umpire who must call a questionable play after three balls and two strikes when the bases are loaded in

the last half of the ninth inning in a tied seventh game of the World Series. (And TV's instant replay is available to everybody but him.)

8. The person who must decide just whose daughters will be next season's debutantes.

9. The roving reporter who drives across town giving us live reports on the path of a tornado.

10. The first person to get on an elevator that has just been repaired.

11. A window washer at the World Trade Center.

12. A joke writer for Joan Rivers. (Who could keep up with her? I can think rapidly, and I can think "risqué," but I cannot think "risqué" rapidly enough for J.R.)

13. The news announcer who must rattle off a roster of the Polish Olympic Swim Team.

14. An interpreter at the United Nations. (Oh, what a temptation!)

15. A third-party candidate for President of the United States. (You'd have to be either an eternal optimist or bored out of your gourd for nothing better to do.)

16. The spokesperson who must interpret what John McEnroe "didn't really say."

17. A proofreader for computer books. (Or worse, a proofreader for cookbooks. You can get away with lousing up a computer, its company, or maybe even its country, but God help you if you botch a recipe.)

18. The Pope's American interpreter (who, I sometimes think, must be the fellow who resigned from the
U.N. because he couldn't resist temptation).

19. The optician who sells spectacle frames to teenage
girls.

20. The person who had to clean out our beef-filled
freezer when we got home from vacation and discovered
that the electricity had been off for two weeks.

But as his father told him, whatever he does for the
rest of his life, he can always say, "At least I don't have to
do *that!*"

42

LOOKING FOR MRS. HERSHEY BAR

Beware the chocolate revolution!

It was bound to happen. When chocolate became so popular that bakeries began making cocoa croissants, delis introduced chocolate cheese, and Italian restaurants featured fudge fettucini and spaghetti chocoletti (now I know why Hershey and Company bought out Skinner Macaroni), it was inevitable that some antichocolate radical would rise up and demand we curtail the cocoa bean.

Last week a journalist, on being asked to review yet one more book on chocolate, wrote: "That's it! Enough! I've had it with chocolate! Like Al Capp's 'schmoos,' chocolate has taken over the world! Office workers nibble on M&M's. School kids sneak Snickers into their lunch sacks. Club members can't hold a meeting without double-fudge brownies. Even hotels now send two chocolate mints to bid you goodnight! I am sick, sick, sick of chocolate!"

Personally, I think that journalist is sick, sick, sick period. As far as I am concerned, anybody who can't stand chocolate must be mentally ill. I'll bet she is one of those crazies who snacks on sunflower seeds and orders fruit and cheese for after-dinner dessert. (I once had a friend like that. Whenever anybody gave Melissa Ann a box of chocolates, she ate all the butter bonbons *first*. Can you imagine that? Nobody was surprised when Melissa Ann went bonkers.)

Like most radicals, that journalist didn't give the chocolate book a fair review. She completely ignored the beautifully constructed phrases ("rich, creamy caramel, thrice-coated with smooth, sweet chocolate and topped with fresh-roasted almonds"), the mouth-watering photographs (what's more aesthetic than dark semisweet chocolate blending with white seven-minute icing?), the exciting new recipes (Godiva Goulash; Hamburger à la Hershey). Instead she went on and on about "chocolate mania," inferring that we are all becoming chocoholics, and insisting that "something be done about it." (You know what that means, don't you? Back to those blah bread donuts!)

I doubt that we are becoming a nation of chocoholics, but as a concerned chocolate lover and founder of the Save the Chocolate Bar Society, I have compiled a quiz to ascertain one's addiction to chocolate. I beg you to take the test, and when you tabulate your score, to act accordingly.

Are You a Chocoholic?

1. When dining in a restaurant, do you scan the dessert menu before you even look at the entrees? (If you ask for the dessert menu before you order a cocktail, score double.)

2. When ordering dessert, do you settle for a single scoop of ice cream (the only thing chocolate on the menu)

when fresh strawberries are in season and the specialty of the house is Shortcake Supreme?

3. Do you accept the fact that when it comes to chocolate, one pound in the mouth means three pounds to the hips? (Do you acknowledge that it's worth it?)

4. Do you vow you won't nibble on a Nestle's before lunch, then decide that *is* lunch?

5. After a harrowing day at the office, do you stop off at the candy machine for just a quick one before you go home? Do you often have more than one?

6. Do you sometimes have "one too many" and find you can't make it through dinner?

7. Do you sneak downstairs late at night for a chocolate "fix," then panic if you open the cookie jar and find nothing there but vanilla wafers and oatmeal crunchies?

8. Do you read articles and books about chocolate just to get a vicarious thrill?

9. Do you buy a lot of baker's chocolate even though you don't bake?

10. When feeling depressed, blue, or just down, do you munch on Milky Ways to perk yourself up? Do you deliberately try to get depressed, blue, or just down so you'll have an excuse to break out the Milky Ways?

11. When someone says "kisses," do you think of "Hershey's" before "his"?

12. Do you feel a surge of justifiable anger when somebody suggests you should cut down on chocolate? (Down with the revolution!)

If you answered "Yes" to six or more of the above, you will be pleased to know that you have passed the test with flying colors and may proudly call yourself a confirmed chocoholic. I assume that you will now want to accept membership in our Save the Chocolate Bar Society. There are no meetings, no minutes, no dues, and only one rule. When ordering desserts, baking goodies, eating snacks, or serving sweets: Think *chocolate!*

As for those of you who failed the test, you deserve your sunflower seeds!

43

SPARE ME THOSE SWEEPSTAKES!

A young man named Sam, on learning that he had just won a multimillion-dollar sweepstakes prize, told a reporter interviewing him on television, "Now I can quit my job and just lay back and think about all the places I'm gonna spend that money!"

He doesn't have to think about it. I'll be happy to tell him all the places he's going to spend that money.

Even before he has heard from his old English teacher ("*Lay* back Samuel? Just what, pray tell, is *back?*"), Sam will get a notice from the Internal Revenue Service informing him that (a) he must pay approximately half of that multimillion to the federal government, (b) he must submit an immediate estimate on interest to be earned on the remaining half, and (c) failure to submit such an estimate will result in a substantial penalty. (Note, Sam, "immediate" means "by last March" and "substantial" means just what it says.)

Hot on the heels of the IRS will be the state revenue service, who will want 20 percent of whatever Sam paid to the IRS, though, of course, the 20 percent is merely based on the amount paid to the IRS; it cannot be deducted therefrom.

Being a sane and sensible citizen, Sam will naturally assume that such incredible taxes are ridiculous and will hire an accountant who, after carefully scrutinizing Sam's financial situation, will notify Sam that he must indeed pay all those taxes and even more, the "even more" being the accountant's fee.

Unconvinced, Sam will undoubtedly seek the advice of an attorney, who will charge Sam another whopping fee to tell him just what jail he will go to if he doesn't listen to his accountant.

In addition to an accountant and an attorney, Sam will need the services of a secretary to field all the calls he will be getting from fund-raisers. (Fund-raisers, like tax collectors, have a direct line into money-dispensing computers.)

Now, I have no doubt that Sam will want to share his wealth with the needy, but unfortunately, by the time he has been hit on by such front-runners as The Freeloaders Foundation and Welfare for the Wealthy, he will be either too disillusioned or too broke to take care of the needy.

And I haven't even mentioned relatives. People who inherit, or win, a great deal of money share one common experience: the sudden appearance of relatives they have never even heard of. I'm not referring here to long-lost cousins; no self-respecting con artist claims to be that anymore. A much more effective approach is: "Hi, old buddy, I know you've never met me, but I'm your half brother!"

In these days of multiple marriages, with kids being his-hers-theirs as well as his due to the fact that his ex-wife left him with her first husband's kids, who knows who their siblings are?

However, such big-money winners as Sam need not be too concerned about the relatives they have never heard of, because before such relatives appear on the scene, the fortune will have been fairly well depleted by the relatives they *have* heard of: sons, daughters, spouses, ex-spouses, and in one case I know, a mother-in-law who wrote a most convincing appeal: "If you send me the money to come visit you, I won't."

I do hope that Sam the sweepstakes winner will be able to hang on to just enough money to pay his last claimant: the employment agency that has to find him another job.

Now you may well wonder how I am so knowledgeable about all the expenses involved in winning a sweepstakes prize. I went through a similar experience last winter, when my neighbor Nancy won a sweepstakes contest. I'm not sure just how much she won, for that matter neither is she, but we concluded the prize must have been huge because by the time she had paid all the taxes, donations, and fees Nancy was only out $126.

Of course this did not include the cost of the thirty-two magazines Nancy had inadvertently ordered, not to mention the cookware, and the cosmetics, and the luggage. But that's okay, because if there is anything that pays better than a well-publicized sweepstakes, it's a word-of-mouth garage sale.

So before you go back to work, Sam, lay front and take inventory!

44

IN THE NATIONAL INTEREST

An investigative reporter who once worked for columnist Jack Anderson recently "revealed" that the Department of Defense has been secretly hiring psychics to assist in such Pentagon activities as searching for Russian subs lurking off our coastline and "remote-viewing" various missile projects. I don't know whether the reporter is against psychics in general, or simply the secrecy involved, but he evidently considered his story a bombshell.

I can't imagine why. Surely a reporter who interned under Jack Anderson should be able to come up with a more important target than the Department of Defense. What ever happened to news revelations truly in the national interest, like Liz Taylor's husbands, or Frank Sinatra's fights, or the trials and tribulations of the Kennedy kids?

Who wants to read about the problems in the Pentagon, for heaven's sake? Frankly, I'm not surprised that that reporter is no longer working for Jack Anderson.

Does anybody really care what goes on at the Pentagon? For that matter, does anybody really know what goes on there? I had a friend who worked at the Pentagon for ten years, and every time somebody asked her what she did there, she replied, "I can't tell you." I assumed her job was "top secret" until she admitted one day that she couldn't tell because she didn't know. She claims she spent most of her time shuffling papers, but I doubt that. I visited her at the Pentagon one day and I think it is more likely that she spent most of her day (a) trying to find her office every morning, (b) trying to find the cafeteria every noon, and (c) trying to find her car every evening.

I was told that the Pentagon does not encourage visitors, and I can see why. I'll be willing to bet there are a zillion of them lost in that labyrinthian maze of walkways and stairways, elevators and escalators, corridors and colonnades. It's a huge place; the building alone takes up twenty-nine acres, which is less than half the amount of land allotted to the parking lot. The vast parking facility is necessary not only because the Pentagon has thirty thousand employees, but also because many of those employees have more than one car in the parking lot. Having been unable to find the one they drove on Monday, they had to bring another car on Tuesday . . . and so on. There is a rumor in one army office that an absentminded colonel got promoted to general on the recommendation of his secretary, who suggested it would be cheaper to qualify the fellow for a chauffeur than to supply him with yet one more car.

Personally, I can't think of a better place to put a bunch of psychics than the Pentagon. When they aren't searching for lurking Russian subs, they could look for all those lost Americans who are wandering around the place trying to find an exit.

Every morning a psychic could stand at each entrance and direct civilian and military personnel to their various offices. Psychics could lead new employees to the lavatories and lunchrooms, and "recall" messengers who took a wrong turn in corridor c2 and can't find their way back. And at closing time psychics could stand at each exit and remind everybody where they had parked their cars.

With enough practice those psychics might even be able to teach mental telepathy to the civilian employees so they could figure out just what those military minds are conjuring up for our future. Better yet, the psychics could teach those military minds how to foresee the future, and thus, perhaps, assure one for all of us.

Meanwhile, I think investigative reporters should forget national defense and get back to topics of national interest. How else are we going to find out just what Barbra Streisand has to be so secretive about?

45

THE GOOD OLD DAYS

My husband, like all those who so frequently refer with fondness to "the good old days," has a lousy memory.

This was made evident again last week when we were driving two of our offspring to college for the start of the fall semester. There must have been ten thousand other cars on the highway (due to an idiotic decree that all university students check in on the same day), and as we became ensnarled in the terrible traffic, my spouse said:

"You know, you and I grew up in a good time."

"What do you mean?" I asked, and he replied:

"Everything was so much simpler in our day, and so much better. Take traffic, for example. When we drove to college, there weren't so many cars, there weren't any awful interstate highways, and we didn't have to endure this kind of frustration!"

"Didn't we?" I asked. "All I seem to recall about highway travel in those days was trying to pass a ten-foot-wide truck on a six-foot-wide highway with a zillion cars coming towards me. Don't you remember those narrow roads that were all curves and hills and no-passing zones? I certainly do! There is a curve in Iowa that shall be forever Teresa because of the number of times I almost died there." (Of course the cars of those days had a lot to do with it; the seats didn't adjust and the windshields were so high I could barely see over the dashboard. The cars of that era may have been well made, but they certainly weren't designed for short people.)

Many people accuse me of being cynical or even contemptuous of the past, but that is not true. I just have a better memory than they do.

For all of you out there who tend to be nostalgic about the past, let me recall a few aspects of "the good old days."

- Remember those bitter cold mornings when you awoke to frost on the bedspread, because your father had not yet stoked the furnace? (You who complain of the cold when you dash downstairs to flick the switch on your thermostat should, just one winter, have to shovel coal into a furnace.)

- Remember wearing coats in the classroom because even though the janitor had stoked the furnace at 4 A.M. the school didn't warm up till noon?

- Remember the sweltering summer afternoons when there was no air-conditioning except at the movie house, where you couldn't afford to go because it cost a quarter and your allowance was only a dime? So you sat on the porch and waved your face with a fan from the funeral parlor; remember? And don't forget the nights that were so hot you slept outside and woke up covered with chigger bites. (Now you

179

live in an air-conditioned home, where movies are brought to you via TV, and you long for "the good old days.")

• Remember when all your clothes were made of nonsynthetic material and everything you wore either itched or scratched and had to be dry-cleaned or, if washed, double-starched, sprinkled, and ironed?

• Remember when telephoning long distance cost a fortune and took forever to get your party and then you could hardly hear him? (Now for two dollars you can call Hong Kong in less than a minute and you complain if they don't answer on the third ring.)

• Remember traveling cross-country by airplane when it took all day to get to your destination and you didn't know which was worse: the turbulence, the layovers, or the noise (from the prop engines) that left you deaf for days? (Last week I flew nonstop to L.A. and got there five minutes before I had left home in Omaha, and I confess I complained because the chateaubriand was too rare and the wine wasn't chilled.)

Yet even as I disparage "the good old days," I admit to a bit of nostalgia for them because I know why they were so "good." We were children, we were teenagers, we were young . . . and our parents paid all the bills.

So take heed, my children, and enjoy these, your "good old days," because believe me, they are numbered.

46

ESSENCE OF MEMORIES

Some time ago, journalist Mike Royko wrote a column on perfumes, specifically one scent called Essence of Chicago. Royko could not understand why anyone would want to smell like a city, particularly Chicago.

Royko missed the point. It was not so much a question of *smelling like* Chicago, as it was of *remembering* Chicago. None of the other senses, not sight, touch, sound, or taste, can bring back a memory so quickly and so vividly as does the sense of smell when it captures a familiar fragrance.

Perfume manufacturers thus were cashing in on a nostalgia craze when they created Essence of Chicago, one whiff of which would remind some sentimentalist of a Chicago childhood, a Great Lakes vacation, or a Windy City romance.

If there were such a thing, I would buy in a minute an Essence of St. Joseph, Missouri. It could be any one of a number of scents: freshly washed sheets sun-drying on my mother's clothesline, the pungent newsprint of my father's office, hot dogs roasting at Bartlett Park's picnic grounds, the fragrance of the lilacs along Lover's Lane. I would buy them all and force my family and friends to smell them forever.

Economically, Essence of Memories makes much better sense (pardon the pun) than modern scents. Just last Christmas my son scraped the bottom of his bank account to buy his fiancée a perfume guaranteed to make her look like Krystle Carrington. It was ridiculous, because twenty years from now, when my son and his wife want to recapture that "essence of courtship," Krystle (and her essence) will have been long forgotten. Better they should buy something like Essence of Pepperoni Pizza. Not only would it bring back memories of the place they spent most of their courtship, but I can practically guarantee that "scent" will be around forever. (I know; my house has smelled like pizza for thirty years.)

If perfume manufacturers really want to cash in on the "sensible scent" idea, I offer the following fragrances:

Aroma of Autumn. Remember the marvelous smell of leaves burning on an autumn evening? You don't? Okay, so maybe you're not old enough. For you, they could have Football Rally Bonfires.

Scent of School Supplies. Nobody can explain it, but everybody will agree that the odor of freshly sharpened pencils, brand-new notebook paper, or a yet-unopened textbook brings back happy memories for all "old students" everywhere, even those who hated school.

Eau de Gymnasium. You must admit that there is no scent quite like it, and certainly none more memorable, than that of the high school gym. I defy anybody to walk into a high school gym and not recall the basketball tournaments, the P.E. classes, the Parent-Teacher conferences, the Christmas parties, the proms, all "memories that bless and burn."

Malodor de Mutton. Has there ever been, or is there yet, a college dormitory cafeteria that does not serve mutton at least once a week?

Glorious (however overpowering) Gardenias. Sales may be limited to middle-aged matrons, but to those of us who admit to such age, one whiff of a gardenia will bring back every college formal we ever attended. (Which may explain why our husbands, however generous with other flowers, never send us gardenias.)

Attar of Baby-After-a-Bath. As any parent can tell you, there is no sweeter scent in the world than that of a baby, freshly bathed, all pink and clean and deliciously fragrant. I get so nostalgic just thinking about it, I'd even settle for Attar of Baby-Before-a-Bath.

Area Ambrosias. Pine trees in northern Minnesota; magnolias in Alabama; cherry blossoms in Washington, D.C.; "waves of amber grain" in Nebraska, Iowa, Kansas, and Missouri; the sea air off South Carolina, Southern California, western Florida, or eastern Maine (different in each area); the crisp aromas of any mountain region; the desert air . . . who wouldn't buy at least one of them?

And what of my own area? Incredible as it may seem (especially to their father), five of our children are still young enough to live at home. As a consequence, I am still assaulted every morning by Essence of Adolescent Bedrooms.

Somehow I doubt that I will ever be nostalgic enough to buy that, but I won't make any promises. I am a sucker for sentiment.

Part Six

Oooo ... There's A Bug in My Book!

47

ANNABELLE S QUERY LETTER

patricia kossmann
editor
doubleday
245 park avenue
new york n y

dear pat

may i call
you pat

we have never
met
but i feel that
i know you
because
my landlady
teresa bloomingdale
speaks of you

more often than
she speaks to
god
and sometimes
in the same sentence
though always
respectfully of
course
i wouldn t want
you to think
that she is
unhappy with her
editor god forbid

my name is
annabelle
and i am an
author
or at least
i will be if
you buy my
book

now in case
you are doubting
that a bug
could write a
book
i beg you to
search your own files
for that bestselling
classic
the life and times of

archy and mehitabel
in which a
cockroach named
archy wrote of
the antics and
alibis of
a re incarnated
queen named
mehitabel the
cat
you may find this
difficult
to believe
but i am archy s
granddaughter
the eldest offspring
of archy s son
julius
a wayward lad who
became such an
embarrassment
to his parents

he kept running
around
in the daylight

he was sent to live
with an
uncle
way out in
nebraska

to everyone s
surprise
julius loved the
prairie life
he settled down
married a roach
from a neighboring
ranch
and fathered me
annabelle

but when i grew
up i decided
the rancher s
life was not
for me
so i ranaway to
the city
and found a
pad
in a big old
house that
is a virtual
paradise
for it has
lots of kids
and thus lots
of crumbs

you can imagine
my surprise
when i discovered
that

190

this is the home
of an old fan of
archy s
and another of
your authors
teresa bloomingdale

incidentally
teresa doesn t
know i live
here
and i d appreciate
it if you
would not mention
that fact
because hard as
this is to
believe
she simply hates
bugs
i am free
to come and
go here
because teresa
is too busy
with her
grandchildren josh and matt
lisa and kate
to pay attention
to the likes
of me
or even the likes
of you

for that matter
and that is why
i am writing
this letter
which isn t easy
let me tell
you when i
can t even reach
the shift key

i could write
in cursive
but i know you
publishers
won t read anything
unless it is
typed

so i must struggle
along with this
ancient machine
i wish you d
pay teresa
more money
so she could
buy a
word processor

you might want
to think about
that

in any event i
happen to

know
that teresa
is supposed to
be writing
a book for you
but i ll tell
you something
pat
that woman has
become so
buggy
if you ll pardon
the expression
about those
grandbabies of
hers
she will never
finish that
book

so i thought
to myself
annabelle old
girl
why not finish
the book for
her

now it is
true
that i ve never
written a
book before

but i ve read
lots of them
and even
eaten a few
so i consider
myself
quite literary

besides
i have a lot
to say
and who else
but doubleday
would consider
a book by a
bug

lest you fear
that your
readers
may be repulsed
by a
roach written
book
let me remind
you
i am not
just
any roach

i am your
very own

archy s
very own
granddaughter

annabelle

48

DEAR FLO—FROM ANNABELLE

dear flo

i am settled
at last
and what a paradise
this is

the house is
full of pets
and kids
who scatter crumbs
from the kitchen
to the bedroom
and back again
its all i can do
to keep the place
eaten up

i almost got
eaten myself

last night when
the family cat
ponced on me
as i was typing
the manuscript for
my book

hey cut that out
i cried
as he caught me
under his paw
and he immediately
jumped back
i dont t think the
dumb cat had
ever heard a
cockroach talk
before

who are you
and what are you
doing here he
asked

and i replied
i am annabelle
the new roach in
residence
and if you must know
i am writing a
book

that s ridiculous
he scoffed

cockroaches can t
write
and certainly not
on typewriters

another dummy i thought
to myself
thank god grandpa
archy isn t around
to hear this

of course cockroaches
can write i said
have you never read
that great classic
archy and mehitabel

mehitabel mehitabel he mused
are you by chance
referring to that
infamous feline who
frolicked through
the alleys of manhattan
leaving litters of
kittens on every
doorstep

the same i said
did you know her

not intimately
he admitted
with a sigh

but i met her
once or twice
she was a lovely
thing but quite
crazy you know
she thought she was
a reincarnation of
the egyptian queen
cleopatra

and wasn't she
i asked
for i had read
grandpa archy s
book many times
and never questioned
the credibility of
mehitabel the cat

good heavens no
he said
mehitabel was
never a queen
she was in fact
marc antony s
cleaning lady
the closest she
ever got to his
bed was on
laundry day
to change the
sheets

how do you know
all this
i asked
don t tell me
you were once
marc antony

no no he said
i was polonius
vice president of
the roman senate
and i know what
you are thinking
how did a good
roman like
me get a danish
name like
polonius
my mother was
a shakespeare buff
but she tended to
get her characters
confused

you knew caesar
then i said
and he replied

i was his closest
advisor
alas i was the one
who told him
not to listen to

that crazy wife
of his
get on down
to the forum
i told him
what could happen
to you among
friends

i said i assume
that was when he
was assassinated

that s when we
were both
assassinated he said
sorrowfully
when too late
i came to my
emperor s aid
brutus stabbed me
with that stiletto
thus creating that
immortal quote
et tu polonius
but how did you
become a cat
i asked

computer error
he explained
when my reincarnation
program was processed

i was inadvertently
entered
as a feline
it hasn t been
too bad
in fact i ve had
an interesting
seven lives
two more to
go
and i can be
re programmed
as a
person

well flo you
can see
what a crazy cat
that is
but he is
the least crazy
of the characters who
live here

i must close now
as my landlady
is due home any
minute
and i must not
let her see me
on her typewriter
or anyplace else
for that matter

i hate to
say this
but i think she s
prejudiced

      love
         annabelle

49

MARGOT THE MOTH

have you met margot
polonius the cat
asked me
the other day
and i said
margot who

margot the moth
he replied
though i must
warn you
she won t admit
she s a moth
she prefers to
think of herself
as a
butterfly

she flutters around
here like

she is ms beautiful
if she ever
stopped long enough
to look in
a mirror
she d drop dead
from sheer shock

polonius i said
patiently
if you ll pardon
the expression you
are being
catty
personally i think
it is rather nice
for a creature
to have a
good self image

it s not margot s
self image
that gets to
me
said polonius
so much as her
self righteousness
she not only
considers herself
ms beautiful
but also ms
perfect
she thinks she s

SENSE AND MOMSENSE

an expert on
everything
especially manners
and morals
and she s constantly
criticizing the
rest of us

that s not true
trilled a voice
behind me
i only criticize
when criticism is
called for

and margot the
magnificent
lighted on the
windowsill

my first impression
was pity
poor margot
what an ugly
old worm she
was
but then she
made the mistake
of opening
her mouth

you must be annabelle
she said much

too sweetly
i wish i had met
you sooner
you could have
accompanied me to
the fashion fair
style show
and perhaps found
something smashing
to replace that
dowdy brown thing
you are wearing
don t you own
anything else
dahling

my boy friend
likes me in
brown
i muttered
wishing i had
said lover
even though
he isn t
at least not yet

what were you
doing at a
style show margot
i asked
lunching perhaps

207

my dear don t
be crass
she said
it s moths who
subsist on fabrics
though god knows
how they
survive
in these days of
synthetics
i was modeling
not nibbling
i am in
great demand
on the fashion
circuit
as there are
few butterflies
who look
like me

i can believe
that said
polonius
but margot was
not listening
her ear was
cocked
toward the
living room

they are at
it again

she said
in disgust

who is at
it again
i asked

and she said
maximilian and
carlotta
can t you hear
them

you mean the
lovebirds i asked
referring to
the parakeets
cheerfully chirping
in their cage

lovebirds indeed
scoffed margot
listen to them
bicker
i don t know
why they re called
lovebirds
they never make love

how do you
know
i asked
and polonius

cried
because she
watches
our margot is
a voyeur

i am not
your margot
shouted the moth
in a very
unbutterfly like
tone
and whatever you
say of those
lovebirds
they never make
love
i ll bet they re
both gay

and with that
scathing pronouncement
margot flew to the
closet
undoubtedly to seek
out an untreated
wool sweater
for remember
she missed lunch

I still don t know
the sexual preferences
of maxim and carlotta

but i am glad
grandpa archy isn t
here to bewail the
purloining of
that lovely word
gay

50

ANNABELLE GOES TO HOLLYWOOD

dear flo

you ll never guess
where i ve
been

cinema city hollywood tinsel town

the old girl
was invited
out to hollywood
to make a
film
so i went along
for the
ride

actually i had
no choice

i was in the
side pocket
of her
suitcase
when she began
to pack
and before i
knew it
i was caught
between a curling
iron and a
cosmetic case

try traveling two
thousand miles
with your rear
end perched
on a still hot
curler
and your snout
pressed
against
passion flower
perfume

as you well
know flo
i hate
flying
especially if
i am stashed
in a colder
than bellybluehell

baggage compartment
with nothing to
eat but tooth
paste and
mascara

not that first
class would
have been
better
the last time
i flew
i got hung
up in a garment
bag across from
the first class
galley
i anticipated surely
lobster for lunch
but what did
they serve
but submarine
sandwiches

and i swear
flo
they were the
same damn
sandwiches i
had snubbed on
a previous flight
only this time

they were
thawed

   i think they
   were better
   frozen

we were met
in l a
by a hollywood type
who looked like
she had stepped
right out of the
sixties

   what with her
   mini skirt t shirt
   and cutesy white
   boots

as a matter of fact
she was out of
the sixties
an establishment
protestor
turned t v
producer
she got dressed
in the sixties and
has been too busy
since to
buy clothes

215

she gave the
old girl
a hollywood hug

god they are kissy kissy
out there

and took us to a
motel
which must have
been booked
by a masochistic
computer

or maybe that
computer just
had me in mind
it was certainly
my kind of
place

but not the
old girl s
she cried
this place is a
dump
and if you don t
believe me
take a look at
what just crawled
out from under the
sink

i thought for a
minute
it was my
cousin louie
but i was
mistaken
i must be
getting humanized
all roaches are
beginning to
look alike

you re right
said the
producer
we ll go
someplace
else

and we moved
uptown to the
hyatt
which was great
for the
old girl
but rotten for
me

they restrict
bugs you see

and i had to
sleep outside
in the alley

next day at
the studio
the old girl
asked
where is my script
and the producer
replied

my dear there s
no script
you do this
ad lib
when we turn
on the cameras
just talk

but i can t
cried the o g
and i almost
died laughing
she s been talking
non stop since
i met her
if a camera can
shut her up
i ll buy it

but the old girl
was game
and gave it her all
and worked like
a drudge
all day long

which we soon learned
is the way they
do things out there
those hollywood crazies
work day and night
and often
till dawn
i don t think
they take time
out to sleep

i mean sleep as
in slumber flo
not sleep as in
sex
that i am sure
they somehow
find time for

i guess the old
girl did okay
in l a
but hollywood sure
went to her
head
she now wears
mini skirts
and rolling stone
shirts
and today ordered
cutesy white boots

but as grandpa
archy would say
wotthehell flo
wotthehell

i did learn
one thing
during my stay
in l a
and that is
you cannot
call a cab
question a bell hop
make a reservation
order a meal
buy
anything at all
or make friends
with some
of the nicest
people
unless you speak
spanish

so
if the old girl
plans to go
back to
tinsel town
i sure hope
she waits until

Oooo ... There's a Bug in My Book!

i have finished
my course from
berlitz

till next time flo

hasta la vista

annabelle

CONCLUSION

Dear Reader:

Forgive me for ending this book so abruptly, but a crisis has arisen at our house and I must take time out to cope with it.

I know you will find this as hard to believe as I did (since we both know what a *perfect* housekeeper I am), but the awful fact is: A bug has been seen in our bathroom! Not a gentle spider, this, or even a wayward ant; this was, as my daughter so aptly put it, "an *ugh* bug!"

My first reaction, of course, was simply to sell the house and move, but that seems rather silly, for only one bug. I am not about to let that irksome creature remain in residence, however, so I am locking up my typewriter temporarily, to devote full time to seeking out that little bugger and smashing him to smithereens.

Then I can in clear conscience return to my typewriter to write my next book.

I'll see you then!

Affectionately,
Teresa

EPILOGUE

dear reader

don t hold your
breath

the idiot locked
me in
her typewriter

now we ll see
who writes
the next
book

with love

    annabelle